Keto Diet After 50

the Complete Ketogenic Blueprint For Seniors with 200 Delectable Recipes to Stay Healthy, Eat, Sleep Well, and Shed Weight | with Foolproof 30-day Keto Meal Plan

Helen C. Johnson

Table of Contents

Chapter 5: Smoothies

Chapter 6: Pork

Chapter 7: Beef and Lamb

Chapter 8: Fish and Seafood

Chapter 9: Staples, Broths, Sauces and Dressings

Chapter 10: Sides and Snacks

Chapter 11: Salads

Appendix 1 Measurement Conversion Chart

Appendix 2 The Dirty Dozen and Clean Fifteen

Introduction

Nowadays Ketogenic diet has been rising in popularity, and for good reason — it is simple and yields significant results. In this diet, the body goes into Ketosis, which means that the majority of its cells, including the brain, use Ketones, resulting from the transformation of fatty acids, as fuel instead of glucose. Whether you want to lose fat, increase energy, enhance brain health, improve your blood sugar levels, or improve your overall health, Keto may be the diet you are looking for. However, before we learn how to start a Keto diet, we must develop a good understanding of what it is and why it is so effective.

The Keto Diet has become more prominent as a popular health choice, not only in obese individuals, but also in healthy adults. A Ketogenic diet typically consists of about 70 to 90 percent of calories from fat, with the remaining 10 to 30 percent of calories coming from a mix of carbohydrates and protein combined. It is a diet that causes the body to release Ketones into the bloodstream. Most cells prefer to use blood sugar, which comes from carbohydrates, as the body's main source of energy. In the absence of circulating blood sugar from food, we start breaking down stored fat into molecules called Ketone bodies. This process is called Ketosis. Once you reach Ketosis, most cells will use Ketone bodies to generate energy until we start eating carbohydrates again. The shift, from using circulating glucose to breaking down stored fat as a source of energy, usually happens over two to four days of eating fewer than 20 to 50 grams of carbohydrates per day. Keep in mind that this is a highly individualized process, and some people need a more restricted diet to start producing enough Ketones.

Macro splits of several different types of meals:

Meal Plan	Protein	Carb	Fat
Mixed Meal	30%	40%	30%
Paleo Meal	40%	20%	40%
Low-Carb Meal	40%	10%	50%
Ketogenic Meal	20%	5%	75%

The Keto diet can be described in many different ways, but the most common definition is that it is a high-fat, low-carb, and low-to-moderate protein diet. However, if you don't know what phrases like "high-fat" and "low-carb" means it is difficult to understand what eating Keto actually looks like.

The simplest way to conceptualize the Keto diet is this: If you restrict carbs to the point that you enter and sustain Ketosis, you are on Keto. Ketosis is a metabolic state in which your body is consistently using and burning a highly efficient alternative fuel called Ketones. To produce Ketones and enter Ketosis, we must continually trigger a process in the liver called Keto genesis. The healthiest way to do this is by limiting carb consumption more than any other low carb diet. This is why this version of the low carb diet is called the "Ketogenic diet" — Its primary objective is to limit carbs to the point that you stimulate Keto genesis and enter nutritional Ketosis. If you're not promoting Ketone production and maintaining Ketosis, then you are technically not on the Keto diet. When a person goes on a Keto diet, they lose a lot of weight. That's just what happens. Keto diet is effective in spurring weight loss and improving cardiovascular health risk factors. The Ketogenic diet isn't a miracle diet for weight loss or a fix for all health problems. For certain people (like those with kidney disease), it can be dangerous. And because it's not a long-term plan, you have to manage your diet carefully after stopping Keto.

Think about how your lifestyle fits with such a restrictive plan, as well as what you're willing to give up temporarily. Let that be your guide to help you determine if the Keto diet is right for you.

Chapter 1: Keto Basics
History and Evolution of the Keto Diet

In the early 1900s, doctors used the Keto diet to control seizures in patients with epilepsy. The diet is based on "healthy fasting" and limits a patient's carbohydrate intake while increasing their fat and protein intake. This type of fasting encourages the body to burn Ketones instead of glucose, a process that proved effective for treating epilepsy in children and adults.

The history of the Keto diet began with Dr. Russell Wilder at the Mayo Clinic 1923. He designed the classic Ketogenic diet, which measures four parts fat for every one-part protein and carb. All other Keto diets are based on this four-to-one macronutrient ratio. The classic Keto diet follows a nutritional plan composed of 90% fats, 6% proteins, and 4% carbs. Meal plans using these portions force the body to use fat instead of carbohydrates for energy. The body then enters a state of Ketosis in which the body continues to burn stored fat, resulting in a buildup of Ketones within the body. Ketones are thought to be an especially healthy alternative fuel source.

Ketogenic diet is rooted in the idea that limiting your carbohydrate intake and consuming fats instead will put your body in a "fasted state" where it will burn Ketones instead of glucose- resulting in better health for you.

The following a meal plan puts the body in a state called Ketosis.

60-75% Fat
15-30% Protein
5-10% Carbs

Your Body primarily chooses to run on glucose (sugar), restricting your carbohydrate intake will cause it to feel that it's starving and will generate a secondary energy source from fat to continue sending glucose to the brain. When you limit your carb supply, your body starts to break down the fat into compounds called Ketones, which are an alternative fuel source that many people, believe has impressive benefits for health and weight management.

The Keto Diet: A Settlement with Fasting

Research shows that fasting can control seizures among epilepsy patients. But the drawback is it came back once the patients returned to their regular diet. It's observed that certain patients had fewer seizures when their blood sugar was lowered from eating a high-fat, low-carb diet. That's why created the Ketogenic diet as a way to mimic the metabolism that fasting produces.

Types of Keto Diets

The Keto diet is a low-carb, high-fat diet. It is known to shift the body's metabolism from a carb-supply mode towards a fat-supply mode. There are many versions of the Keto diet, including:

- **The Standard Keto Diet**

This is a very low-carb, moderate-protein, high-fat diet. It usually contains 75% fats, 20% proteins, and 5% carbohydrates.

- **The Cyclic Keto Diet**

This diet involves adhering to a standard Keto diet for five to six days per week followed by one to two days of higher carb consumption, called "refeeding days," which are meant to replenish your body's depleted glucose reserves.

- **The Targeted Keto Diet**

This is a diet that will allow you to add carbs when you have hard workouts.

- **The High-Protein Keto Diet**

This is similar to the standard Keto diet, but it has a high proportion of proteins. The ratio is often 60% fat, 5% carbs, and 35% proteins.

- **Vegan Keto diet**

The vegan Keto diet is for individuals who want to follow a high-fat, low-carb diet, but do not consume animal products. This can be difficult to achieve, as many Keto dieters rely on animal products for a large portion of their diet. Common protein sources for vegan Keto dieters include tofu, tempeh, nuts and nut butters, and beans and legumes in moderate amounts. Though challenging, a vegan Keto diet isn't impossible—it just takes a lot of advance planning.

It is important to know that the favorable Keto diet for people over 50 is the standard Keto diet. Cyclic and targeted Keto diets are more advanced and are often used by athletes and bodybuilders.

Keto–the Low Carb Diet for people over 50 years

Nutritional needs change as we age and a low carb diet could improve your physical and mental health later in life. Our bodies are always changing from the moment we are born. What our bodies require at each stage of our life differs vastly, and it is important to know how to nourish ourselves accordingly for optimal health and well-being.

At the age of 50+ years, our metabolism, nutritional needs and digestive systems have changed a lot and the same diet we followed when we were young adults may not be the best, or healthiest, choice anymore. Our direction in this article is to explain the health benefits of a low carb diet in older age as well as to address other things to consider about nutrition when you reach later stages of life. Keep reading for health insights, tips, and products that are useful for older adults and especially those coping with certain physical conditions.

What Happens to Our Bodies When We Age?

As we age, there are a few key changes that happen to the body that we should be mindful of when it comes to food and nutrition. These are described below.

- **Our metabolism slows down.**

Your metabolism is the amount of energy that your body burns (or the rate at which it breaks down food) in order to function and maintain itself. As we age, our metabolism slows as much as 10% every decade after age 20. So, by the time you reach age 60, your metabolism has slowed down by nearly 40% since your refrigerator-raiding teenage years! If you are age 60 or older, you have probably already noticed a decrease in your appetite. Some people go from

having three meals a day to just two, or smaller more frequent meals and snacks.

So, what does this mean? With a slower metabolism, the body absorbs nutrients from foods at a slower rate, meaning that we should focus on more nutrient-dense foods as we get older. In addition, it can be easier to put on pounds and harder to lose weight. Even if you don't eat much more than usual, the body will store any excess calories that it is unable to burn in the form of fat. Having a higher body fat percentage can create several health problems and increase your risk for things like diabetes and heart disease.

- **Lose muscle mass.**

Another not-so-nice thing that happens when we age is that we tend to lose muscle mass. Muscle mass is important for mobility and strength, but also, having more muscle mass can increase your natural metabolic rate since muscles burn more energy than fat.

Maintaining muscle mass is one of the keys to preventing excessive weight gain in older age, which we mentioned previously is more likely to occur due to slowing metabolic rates. However, it can be challenging to lose weight and build muscle later in life, which is why a healthy diet and daily exercise regimen become even more important around mid-life, if not earlier. Inactivity can accelerate muscle loss that already begins to occur around age 30.

Eating lean protein and incorporating resistance training (anything that requires the muscles to work against gravity, weights or rubber resistance bands) are all good ideas to help maintain or increase muscle mass. However, one thing to note about protein consumption in older age is that due to our slowing metabolism, animal proteins may not be broken down as easily. Instead, reach for plant-based proteins or grass-fed or marine collagen, which are a bit easier on the digestive system. Furthermore, research has shown that the amino acid profiles of animal proteins can trigger certain enzymes in the body that have negative effects on aging. Don't worry about cutting out animal protein altogether, but opt for things like vegan protein shakes, tofu or tempeh more frequently.

- **High risk of cardiovascular diseases.**

Our heart and blood vessels become "stiffer" as we get older, meaning that our blood flow is slower and our blood pressure tends to increase. That said, the heart still functions well, but it may have to work harder to pump more blood when we exercise or become ill. Regular aerobic exercise (anything that gets your heart rate up and oxygen flowing, such as running, walking and swimming) can all contribute to improved heart health and athletic performance in seniors. In addition, plaque from years of unhealthy eating can build up and exacerbate blood pressure problems. The good news is that this can be reversed, mainly through making changes in the diet. Avoid sugar and trans-fats while increasing your fibre intake as well as healthy fats and lean protein. Do not rely on medications such as aspirin to provide bandage solutions for poor lifestyle habits.

- **Fat Infiltration**

After the age of 50, the process of fat infiltrating your muscles accelerates. Fat infiltration also increases with inactivity. The effect of this is you may feel easily fatigued. However, research shows that resistance training can mitigate this as it increases lean muscle mass and may improve muscle composition.

- **Menopause**

During menopause, women may experience an increase in body fat. When women are younger, they tend to collect fat around their hips and thighs. This is known as gynoid fat distribution.

However, as women enter perimenopause and menopause, the fat distribution pattern changes. Fat starts accumulating around the abdomen. This pattern is called android fat distribution that is common in males. These changes are a result of hormonal changes. Menopause in a woman officially starts when she has not received her menstrual period for about 12 months. During menopause, a woman's estrogen levels are generally lower. Reduction in estrogen levels has been linked to an increase in body fat.

8 Benefits of the Keto diet

A Keto diet is basically a high-fat, very low-carb, and moderate-protein diet. A Keto diet requires that you cut on carbs and increase your fat consumption to help the body burn up the fat in its stores more efficiently. Keto diet acknowledge how hard low carb eating plans are to keep up. But they also believe that the health benefits and general good body vibes far outweigh having to say no to doughnuts.

1. **Keto diet and weight loss**

Weight loss is one of the main reasons people choose to diet. The Keto diet promotes weight loss in multiple ways. Processed and refined carbs can contribute to weight gain. By reducing your intake or cutting them out of your diet, you're removing a key cause of weight gain. There's also evidence that a Keto diet suppresses appetite. Did you know you get hungry because of hormones your body releases? You do now. Keto foods may make your body release less of these hormones.

2. **Diabetes management**

A Keto diet may help people with diabetes manage certain aspects of the condition more effectively. In super-simplified terms, diabetes is a chronic health condition that messes with your body's ability to turn food into energy. You may have heard that the price of insulin is going up and that this is very bad news for people with diabetes. Insulin's job is to break down glucose and other blood sugars. The bodies of folks with type 1 diabetes don't produce enough insulin, so they need regular doses of it from an outside source. Some people with type 1 diabetes have turned to dietary solutions to reduce their insulin needs. Some studies have suggested that Ketogenic diets may be particularly helpful. Keto and other low carb eating plans lower blood sugar levels, so your body needs less insulin. People with type 1 diabetes aren't the only ones who may reap the benefits. In a small 2008 study of people with type 2 diabetes, 95 percent of participants who followed a Keto diet reported reducing or eliminating glucose-lowering medication in the first 6 months. If you have diabetes, it's important to talk with your doctor before starting or stopping the Keto diet, because the dietary change could have drastic effects on your blood sugar.

3. **Keto diet and cholesterol**

The Keto diet might help lower your cholesterol. There are two kinds of cholesterol in your body: high-density lipoprotein (HDL), which is the "good" cholesterol, and low-density lipoprotein (LDL), which is the "bad" cholesterol. Lipoproteins carry fat around your body. LDLs pick it up, and then HDLs take the fat-laden LDLs to your liver so they can be flushed out of your system. A Keto diet may help you make sure there's more HDL than LDL circulating in your body. A 2012 review suggested that the Keto diet could boost levels of HDL cholesterol in the bloodstream (although it didn't dramatically reduce LDL levels). According to some older research, healthy fats can be great for boosting your HDL levels. So it's not surprising that low carb, high fat diets can help keep cholesterol levels in check. But the key word here is "healthy" — stick to mostly unsaturated fats, found in foods like avocado, nuts, fatty fish, and olive oil. Saturated fats, which are found in butter and many fried foods, can increase cholesterol.

4. Reducing acne symptoms

While acne isn't life-threatening, it can be traumatic to live with (especially in adults). Skin conditions like acne can cause all sorts of psychological issues for folks who live with them. Many treatments are available for acne. Some involve creams and medications, and some can be quite invasive and painful. But possible links between diet and dermatology may be helpful in managing acne and other conditions. There may be a link between blood sugar and skin health. Processed and refined carbs can mess with your gut bacteria (the good kind of bacteria that we feed with yogurt, not the bad kind we try to kill with medicine). If your gut bacteria get out of whack, it can wreak havoc on your blood sugar levels. And that can be bad for your skin. For example, research suggests diabetes can cause skin symptoms. As we've mentioned, Keto diets are pretty darn nifty if you want to rein in your blood sugar levels. A 2012 review suggested that the Keto diet might be helpful in managing acne. More research is needed, but results so far have been promising.

5. Reducing cancer risk

There's been a bunch of research into Keto diets and cancer treatment. Keeping the carbs low could have a few different effects to help reduce your cancer risk. For one thing, restricting carbs could cause more oxidative stress in cancer cells than in regular cells. This is super helpful alongside chemotherapy and radiotherapy when the goal is to kill cancer cells while leaving as many healthy cells intact as possible. Another benefit of the Keto diet is lowering blood sugar levels, which can starve some cancerous cells of energy. During Ketosis, your liver burns fat and produces Ketones. Because some cancer cells aren't good at metabolizing Ketones, they die when there's no glucose around for energy. Relying on Ketone bodies for energy instead of glucose and unhealthy fats leads to a drop in blood sugar levels. In certain types of cancer, this can result in the starvation and death of cancer cells.

6. Boosting your brainbox

Your squishy blood pump isn't the only essential organ that may benefit from a dip into the Keto lifestyle. There's also evidence that a brief carb fast can be good for the brain. A 2012 review of studies suggested there may be a link between Ketones and the overall strength and health of nerve cells. This has potentially huge ramifications for the Keto diet as a treatment for degenerative neurological conditions like Alzheimer's. As with many aspects of the Keto diet, more research is needed on this, but some results have been promising.

7. Keto diet and seizures (including the epileptic kind)

There is increasing evidence that a Ketogenic diet could help people with conditions like epilepsy manage their seizures. A 2019 review suggests that the Keto diet might be a good alternative for managing epilepsy in people who don't respond to medications. The review also mentions that people have used fasting to manage epilepsy for ages, so the Keto diet may be a less restrictive option.

8. Keto diet and PCOS

Polycystic ovary syndrome (PCOS) is a hormonal disorder. It can lead to excess male hormones and cysts on the ovaries (meaning they don't function as they should). A 2005 pilot study suggested that a Keto diet could help with PCOS complications like weight gain or loss, hormone balance, and insulin levels in wom who had both obesity and PCOS.

•   The Keto Diet is Created for Weight Loss

A true Ketogenic diet for weight loss contains 80% fat, fewer than 5% carbs, and 15-20% protein. To achieve these percentages, dieters must ditch a few carbohydrate-heavy food groups, including grains, dairy, beans, and fruits, and load up on meat, fish, butter, eggs, avocados, oils, nuts, seeds and non-starchy vegetables. Eating greater amounts of protein while on the Keto diet might help keep your hunger at bay. In addition to weight loss, Ketogenic diets have also been shown to offer several other health benefits.

The Keto diet may help patients:

- Improve cognitive functioning
- Reduce inflammation from high blood sugar
- Slow the spread of various cancers
- Reduce sugar addictions
- Increase female fertility
- If you're aiming for rapid and permanent weight loss (or any of the other health benefits mentioned), the Keto diet may be for you. It also continues to be effective in decreasing epileptic seizures.

Keto Diet Tips for Seniors

At the heart of a Ketogenic diet is Ketones. When the body is low on blood sugar, it produces Ketones from fat as an alternative energy source. Production of Ketones happens when you cut on your carb intake and take the right amount of protein.

Here are 10 tips on how to get the best out of a Keto diet for people over 50:

9. Don't Skimp on Protein

Protein is an essential component on the Keto diet menu for women over 50. For weight loss, consuming the right amount of protein is crucial. Protein is vital as it helps increase muscle mass and prevent a metabolic slowdown. In fact, protein boosts metabolism. This macronutrient has a higher thermic effect on food (30 to 50%) than other nutrients. The thermic effect of food refers to the number of calories required to digest and metabolize the food. Protein also regulates the hunger hormone ghrelin. It causes a reduction in the production of ghrelin, leaving you full for longer. So after eating a high protein breakfast, it is unlikely that you will reach for a snack before your next meal. The recommended amount of protein is 0.8 grams per kilogram of body weight per day. If you weigh 90kgs, the minimum amount of protein you should consume in a day is about 72 grams. To avoid poor muscle growth, also ensure you consume the right amount of protein.

10. Get the Right Amount of Fats

The whole point of a Keto for Women Over 50 is to cut back on the carbs while getting the right amounts of fats. One of the best parts about Keto eating is that you get to eat fats at every meal. However, once you become fat-adapted, you might end up over consuming fats. If you want to cut weight, you have to use up the fat stores in your body instead of getting all your calories from fats. Dr. Bret Scher suggests that before your body becomes fat-adapted, it is okay to eat high amounts of healthy fats . When you become fat-adapted and can go a long time without eating, you should regulate those amounts. The secret is to keep watch of your fat consumption. But if you hit a weight stall, you might want to check and make sure you are not consuming too many fats. Ensure that you cut back on fats without sacrificing fullness or prompting the return of cravings for salty or sugary ultra-processed foods. Also, do not starve yourself; just watch out for the excess fat.

11. Manage Stress

Stress is an outright enemy of weight loss. When you are under stress, the body causes the release of cortisol. This sends your body in a flight or fight mode, temporarily pausing under process in the body and slowing your metabolism. While cortisol is an important hormone, in excess, it can be harmful. Cortisol may cause hunger and increase your appetite. It may also cause cravings for sugary, fatty, and salty foods. This means you will likely forget about your Keto-friendly foods and grab some french fries, burgers, or pizza. You have heard about stress eating. It is an actual phenomenon, and under stress, you may end up overeating. Consequently, you may abandon your Ketogenic diet without even realizing it. And while you are in your 50s, there are many things to stress about – your kids, home, friends, and relatives. Even worrying about your weight loss is a bad thing. But remember, stressful conditions are detrimental to your weight loss. Try to take some time off things and relax.

12. Cut Back On Alcohol

Alcohol contains many extra calories making it a key contributor to weight gain if you drink a lot. An occasional glass of wine or beer does not hurt. However, overdrinking has a negative effect on weight loss. When you consume alcohol, your body's metabolic priority changes. The body puts on pause the metabolism of other substances to metabolize alcohol. This is because the body wants to get rid of a toxic byproduct of alcohol called acetate. Even while on a Keto diet, taking alcohol in excess is counterproductive. So if you have reached a stall and you cannot seem to lose any more weight, it might be best to cut back on the booze.

13. Get Plenty Of Quality Sleep

During menopause that takes place between 40 and 50, it is common to experience sleep disturbances . Poor sleep has been associated with positive energy balance which could cause weight gain over time. So in the case you have reached a plateau, check whether you are getting quality sleep.

Getting an inadequate amount of sleep may also increase the release of the primary stress hormone called cortisol linked to abdominal fat. To get better sleep, try going to bed at the same time every day. Also, sleep in a dark room and avoid drinking alcohol or eating right before bed.

Tips for better sleep include:

1. Sleep in a cool, dark room.

2. Wear earplugs and eyeshades.

3. Limit screen time and blue light before bed (or try the glasses that block blue light).

4. Go to bed and get up at the same time each day.

5. Stop drinking coffee by noon and limit caffeine consumption in all forms.

6. Avoid alcohol before bed.

7. Get exposure to natural daylight each day.

1. Cut Back On Carbs

For Keto for women over 50 to be effective, you have to limit the number of carbs you consume. But once you have been following your Keto diets, carbs may creep back in. This is mostly in the form of nuts, fruits, and sauces.

You need to check your carbs intake then cut back to consuming under 20 grams of net carbs a day. Be on the lookout to avoid processed foods rich in carbs, such as bagels, breakfast cereals, pastries, and waffles.

2. Experiment With Inter**mittent Fasting**

Once your body is fat-adapted and you can go for long hours without eating, you can try intermittent fasting. With Intermittent fasting, an individual alternates between long periods of fasting and eating. An individual usually goes without food for about 16 to 24 hours.

A key rule of low-carb eating is to eat only when you are hungry and not to a specific eating schedule as many people are accustomed to. You can try a 24 hour fast where you eat dinner tonight then eat again at dinner the following day.

Alternatively, you can skip breakfast then eat lunch and dinner with an 8-hour interval in between. You can switch up the two methods by doing a 16:8 fast followed by a 24 hour fast then a day of normal eating. Do not go for long fasts that run for several days. And always discuss with your doctor first, as fasting is not safe for everyone.

3. Lift Weights More

Starting yourself on a diet is usually not enough for weight loss. To burn calories and shed weight, you need to combine exercise and dieting. To achieve maximum weight loss, a combination of Keto and exercises for women over 50 is necessary.

Weight training (sometimes referred to as strength or resistance training) helps build muscle mass. Muscle plays a crucial role in metabolism as increased lean muscle mass boosts your body's metabolism. With strength training, your resting metabolic rate increases, and your body burns more calories at rest.

Weight lifting does not have to be excessive – about 90 seconds per muscle group at least twice weekly should be enough. Ensure that the weights you are lifting are heavy enough such that after 20 to 15 reps, you cannot do one more. Ensure you drink enough water after your workouts. Also, include rest days in between heavy exercise so that your body can recover.

4. Avoid Added Sugars

Limiting foods high in artificial sugars such as soda, candy, cookies, sugary cereals is crucial for weight loss. Also, if you have been adding artificial sweeteners such as sucralose to your low-carb diet you may want to wean them off as they can lead to unhelpful sugar cravings.

Given that such foods are sweet they are easy to overeat and can take you back a few steps when you are trying to cut weight. Always read labels to check whether an item has added sugars on the nutrition facts. You can also check the ingredient list for common sweeteners such as agave, corn syrup, or cane sugar.

5. **Set Achievable Goals**

Having realistic achievable goals is important for anyone trying to shed some weight. Most women have an idealized weight goal they have never been able to achieve. This number usually has no relationship to their well-being and health.

Most women often think of how they want to be instead of the impact of fat loss on their overall health. Yet thinking of weight as just the number you see on the scale is self-sabotage. If you are in the habit of hopping on the scale every day, you should stop. Try and look beyond the scale. Instead focus on how great you feel, how many inches you have lost around your weight, and how your clothes fit. Keep a positive mindset and do not get discouraged as weight loss can be frustrating. Remember the long-term goal is to lose fat, adapt to a healthier lifestyle and improve your overall health.

Chapter 2: Following Keto

The brain is a hungry organ that consumes lots of energy every day, and it can't run on fat directly. It can only run on glucose – or Ketones. On a Ketogenic diet, the entire body switches its fuel supply to run mostly on fat, burning fat all day long. When insulin levels drop very low, fat burning can increase dramatically. It becomes easier to access your fat stores to burn them off. This is great if you're trying to lose weight, but there can also be other benefits, such as less hunger and a steady supply of energy — without the sugar peaks and valleys that often occur when eating high-carb meals. This may help keep you alert and focused. When the body produces Ketones, it enters a metabolic state called Ketosis. The fastest way to get there is by fasting – not eating anything – but nobody can consistently fast forever.

A Keto diet, on the other hand, also results in Ketosis and can be eaten indefinitely. It has many of the benefits of fasting – including weight loss – without having to fast long term. The Ketogenic diet is a popular, effective way to lose weight and improve your health. When followed correctly, this low-carb, high-fat diet will raise blood Ketone levels. These provide a new fuel source for your cells and cause most of the unique health benefits of this diet. On a Ketogenic diet, your body undergoes many biological adaptations, including a reduction in insulin levels and increased fat breakdown.

When this happens, your liver starts producing high numbers of Ketones to supply energy for your brain. However, it can often be hard to know whether you're in Ketosis or not.

Foods to Eat in Keto Diet

You should base the majority of your meals around these foods:

- Meat: red meat, steak, ham, sausage, bacon, chicken, and turkey
- fatty fish: salmon, trout, tuna, and mackerel
- Eggs: pastured or omega-3 whole eggs
- Butter and cream: grass-fed butter and heavy cream
- Cheese: unprocessed cheeses like cheddar, goat, cream, blue, or mozzarella
- Nuts and seeds: almonds, walnuts, flaxseeds, pumpkin seeds, chia seeds, etc.
- Healthy oils: extra virgin olive oil, coconut oil, and avocado oil
- Avocados: whole avocados or freshly made guacamole
- Low carb veggies: green veggies, tomatoes, onions, peppers, etc.
- Condiments: salt, pepper, herbs, and spices
- It's best to base your diet mostly on whole, single-ingredient foods.

Foods to Avoid in Keto Diet

Any food that's high in carbs should be limited. Here's a list of foods that need to be reduced or eliminated on a Ketogenic diet:

- Sugary foods: soda, fruit juice, smoothies, cake, ice cream, candy, etc.
- Grains or starches: wheat-based products, rice, pasta, cereal, etc.
- fruit: all fruit, except small portions of berries like strawberries
- Beans or legumes: peas, kidney beans, lentils, chickpeas, etc.
- Root vegetables and tubers: potatoes, swee

- potatoes, carrots, parsnips, etc.
- low fat or diet products: low fat mayonnaise, salad dressings, and condiments
- Some condiments or sauces: barbecue sauce, honey mustard, teriyaki sauce, ketchup, etc.
- Unhealthy fats: processed vegetable oils, mayonnaise, etc.
- Alcohol: beer, wine, liquor, mixed drinks
- Sugar-free diet foods: sugar-free candies, syrups, puddings, sweeteners, desserts, etc.

10 Signs and Symptoms that You Are in Ketosis

Several key signs and symptoms can help you identify whether you are in Ketosis. Ultimately, if you're following the guidelines of a Ketogenic diet and stay consistent, you should be in some form of Ketosis. If you want a more accurate assessment, monitor Ketone levels in your blood, urine or breathe on a weekly basis.

That being said, if you're losing weight, enjoying your Ketogenic diet and feeling healthier, there is no need to obsess over your Ketone levels.

Here are 10 common signs and symptoms of Ketosis, both positive and negative.

1. Bad breath

People often report bad breath once they reach full Ketosis. It's actually a common side effect. Many people on Ketogenic diets and similar diets, such as the Atkins diet, report that their breath takes on a fruity smell. This is caused by elevated Ketone levels. The specific culprit is acetone, a Ketone that exits the body in your urine and breath. While this breath may be less than ideal for your social life, it can be a positive sign for your diet. Many Ketogenic dieters brush their teeth several times per day or use sugar-free gum to solve the issue. If you're using gum or other alternatives like sugar-free drinks, check the label for carbs. These may raise your blood sugar levels and reduce Ketone levels.

2. Weight loss

Ketogenic diets, along with normal low-carb diets, are highly effective for weight loss. As dozens of weight loss studies have shown, you will likely experience both short- and long-term weight loss when switching to a Ketogenic diet. Fast weight loss can occur during the first week. While some people believe this to be fat loss, it's primarily stored carbs and water being used up. After the initial rapid drop in water weight, you should continue to lose body fat consistently as long as you stick to the diet and remain in a calorie deficit.

3. Increased Ketones in the blood

One of the hallmarks of a Ketogenic diet is a reduction in blood sugar levels and an increase in Ketones. As you progress further into a Ketogenic diet, you will start to burn fat and Ketones as the main fuel sources. The most reliable and accurate method of measuring Ketosis is to measure your blood Ketone levels using a specialized meter. It measures your Ketone levels by calculating the amount of beta-hydroxybutyrate (BHB) in your blood.

This is one of the primary Ketones present in the bloodstream. According to some experts on the Ketogenic diet, nutritional Ketosis is defined as blood Ketones ranging from 0.5–3.0 mmol/L. Measuring Ketones in your blood is the most accurate way of testing and is used in most research studies. However, the main downside is that it requires a small pinprick to draw blood from your finger. What's more, test kits can be expensive. For this reason, most people will just perform one test per week or every other week. If you would like to try testing your Ketones, Amazon has a good selection available.

4. Increased Ketones in the breath or urine

Another way to measure blood Ketone levels is a breath analyzer. It monitors acetone, one of the three main Ketones present in your blood during Ketosis. This gives you an idea of your body's Ketone levels since more acetone leaves the body when you are in nutritional Ketosis. The use of acetone breath analyzers has been shown to be fairly accurate, though less accurate than the blood monitor method.

Another good technique is to measure the presence of Ketones in your urine on a daily basis with special indicator strips. These also measure Ketone excretion through the urine and can be a quick and cheap method to assess your Ketone levels each day. However, they're not considered very reliable.

5. Appetite suppression

Many people report decreased hunger while following a Ketogenic diet. The reasons why this happens are still being investigated. However, it's been suggested that this hunger reduction may be due to an increased protein and vegetable intake, along with alterations to your body's hunger hormones. The Ketones themselves may also affect your brain to reduce appetite.

6.   Increased focus and energy

People often report brain fog, tiredness and feeling sick when first starting a very low-carb diet. This is termed the "low carb flu" or "Keto flu." However, long-term Ketogenic dieters often report increased focus and energy. When you start a low-carb diet, your body must adapt to burning more fat for fuel, instead of carbs. When you get into Ketosis, a large part of the brain starts burning Ketones instead of glucose. It can take a few days or weeks for this to start working properly.

Ketones are an extremely potent fuel source for your brain. They have even been tested in a medical setting to treat brain diseases and conditions such as concussion and memory loss. Therefore, it comes as no surprise that long-term Ketogenic dieters often report increased clarity and improved brain function. Eliminating carbs can also help control and stabilize blood sugar levels. This may further increase focus and improve brain function.

7.   Short-term fatigue

The initial switch to a Ketogenic diet can be one of the biggest issues for new dieters. Its well-known side effects can include weakness and fatigue. These often cause people to quit the diet before they get into full Ketosis and reap many of the long-term benefits. These side effects are natural. After several decades of running on a carb-heavy fuel system, your body is forced to adapt to a different system.

As you might expect, this switch doesn't happen overnight. It generally requires 7–30 days before you are in full Ketosis. To reduce fatigue during this switch, you may want to take electrolyte supplements. Electrolytes are often lost because of the rapid reduction in your body's water content and the elimination of processed foods that may contain added salt. When adding these supplements, try to get 1,000 mg of potassium and 300 mg of magnesium per day.

8.   Short-term decreases in performance

As discussed above, removing carbs can lead to general tiredness at first. This includes an initial decrease in exercise performance. It's primarily caused by the reduction in your muscles' glycogen stores, which provide the main and most efficient fuel source for all forms of high-intensity exercise. After several weeks, many Ketogenic dieters report that their performance returns to normal. In certain types of ultra-endurance sports and events, a Ketogenic diet could even be beneficial. What's more, there are further benefits — primarily an increased ability to burn more fat during exercise.

One famous study found that athletes, who had switched to a Ketogenic diet burned as much as 230% more fat when they exercised, compared to athletes who were not following this diet. While it's unlikely that a Ketogenic diet can maximize performance for elite athletes, once you become fat-adapted it should be sufficient for general exercise and recreational sports (20Trusted Source).

9.   Digestive issues

A Ketogenic diet generally involves a major change in the types of foods you eat. Digestive issues such as constipation and diarrhea are common side effects in the beginning.

Some of these issues should subside after the transition period, but it may be important to be mindful of different foods that may be causing digestive issues. Also, make sure to eat plenty of healthy low-carb veggies, which are low in carbs but still contain plenty of fiber. Most importantly, don't make the mistake of eating a diet that lacks diversity. Doing that may increase your risk of digestive issues and nutrient deficiencies.

10. Insomnia

One big issue for many Ketogenic dieters is sleep, especially when they first change their diet. A lot of people report insomnia or waking up at night when they first reduce their carbs drastically. However, this usually improves in a matter of weeks. Many long-term Ketogenic dieters claim that they sleep better than before after adapting to the diet.

Avoiding the Keto Flu

In the beginning, some people experience the "Keto flu" when they are transitioning into Ketosis. Many people who begin the ketosis process for the first time get flu-like symptoms, feel like all their energy is drained, and basically just feel awful. The primary reason people get Keto flu is because their electrolytes get out of balance.

- Drink a lot of water. You need to be drinking atleast half your body weight in ounces per day.

- Use Pink Himalayan Rock Salt. About 1 tsp. per day should do the trick. A simple trick is to put 1 tsp. of pink sea salt in a bowl on the counter. By the end of the day, make sure you have used up the entire teaspoon. Himalayan salt has more minerals and trace elements than other salts. It's also a very pure and unprocessed product. Sodium is an important electrolyte, so this is the perfect way to get high-quality salt in your diet (stay far away from white table salt)!

- CALM. Magnesium not only helps combat stress in the body, but it's an important mineral that's required for more than 700 biochemical reactions in your body.

- Homemade Bone Broth. This will help balance the vitamins and minerals in your body in the most incredible way. Broth is amazing for healing and promoting a healthy digestive tract, reducing joint pain and inflammation, and promoting hair and nail growth (and some say it can help with cellulite because it helps maintain the integrity of the cell walls!).

Additional Supplements

In addition to the supplements listed above for avoiding the keto flu, I recommend taking the following supplements. These are optional and not required.

- MCT Oil – This will help you to get into ketosis faster. MCT stands for Medium-Chain Triglycerides. It's basically a refined version of coconut oil that is 6x more potent.

- Start with 1 tsp. and build from there up to 1 tbsp. I usually add 1 tbsp. (with some grass-fed butter) in the morning to my bulletproof coffee! You'll love what it does for your mental clarity.

- You can get MCT oil at health food stores, nutritional supplement stores, online, and even at some well-stocked grocery stores.

- Probiotics – Did you know that up to 70% of your immune system resides in your gut? Probiotics can help restore balance back to your digestive system and provide an overall boost to your immune system.

- The bacteria in your body out number your cells by more than 10 to 1. Remember, the good bacteria help to keep you in check. They help to fight against the "bad" bacteria, viruses, and other pathogens.

- It's really important to give this good bacteria an extra hand because the toxins, chemicals, and any antibiotics we are exposed to will kill off these microscopic warriors.

- Omega 3s (Fish Oil) – Omega 3s help reduce inflammation in the body, increase your ability to burn fat, strengthen your immune system, improve circulation, improve good cholesterol, and the list goes on and on.

- Rhodiola – If you live a high-stress life, rhodiola can help combat some of the effects. It helps fight fatigue, boosts memory, and increase work capacity to improve productivity.

Relevance of Exercise in Healthy Life Style

You lose muscle mass as you get older, and exercise can help you rebuild it. Muscles also burn more calories than fat, even at rest, which will offset your slowing metabolism. Exercise helps stop, delay, and sometimes improve serious illness like heart disease, high blood pressure, diabetes, stroke, Alzheimer's disease, arthritis, and osteoporosis. It can help your brain stay sharp and keep you from falling into a funk.

Types of Exercise

Young or old, everyone needs different kinds. Cardio or aerobic exercise gets your heart rate up and makes you breathe harder, which builds your endurance and burns calories. Strength or weight training keeps your muscles ready for action. Flexibility exercises help you stay limber so you can have a full range of movement and avoid injury. Balance training becomes important after age 50, so you can prevent falls and stay active.

Choose the Right Activities

Some activities provide more than one type of exercise, so you'll get more bang from your workout buck. Definitely pick things that you enjoy doing! Your doctor or physical therapist can suggest ways to adapt sports and exercises, or better alternatives, based on the limitations of any medical conditions you have.

1. **Walking**

Simple and effective! It builds your stamina, strengthens lower body muscles, and helps fight against bone diseases like osteoporosis. It's easy to work into your day. You can go solo or make it social. At a moderate pace, you'll get exercise and still be able to chat with a friend or group.

2. **Jogging**

If you like to sweat a bit more when you exercise, try jogging to get your heart rate up. As long as you take it slow and steady, wear the right shoes, and take walking breaks, your joints should be fine. Soft surfaces, like a track or grass, may also help. Pay attention to your calves and hips, with extra stretching and strengthening to lessen your chance of injuries.

3. **Dancing**

It doesn't really matter what kind: ballroom, line, square, even dance-based aerobics classes like Zumba and Jazzercise. Dancing helps your endurance, strengthens your muscles, and improves your balance. It burns a lot of calories because it gets you moving in all directions. Research shows learning new moves is really good for your brain, too. Plus, you could be having so much fun, you might not notice you're doing exercise.

4. **Golfing**

Much of the benefit of this sport comes from the walking: an average round is more than 10,000 steps, or about 5 miles! In addition, your swing uses your whole body, and it requires good balance -- and calm focus. If you carry or pull your clubs, that's even more of a workout. But even using a cart is worth it. You're still working your muscles and getting in steps along with fresh air and stress relief.

5. **Tennis**

Racquet sports, including tennis, squash, and badminton, may be particularly good at keeping you alive longer and for lowering your chance of dying from heart disease. Playing tennis 2 or 3 times a week is linked to better stamina and reaction times, lower body fat, and higher "good" HDL cholesterol. And it builds bones, especially in your arm, low back, and neck. Play doubles for a less intense, more social workout.

6. **Cycling**

It's especially good when you have stiff or sore joints, because your legs don't have to support your weight. The action gets your blood moving and builds muscles on both the front and back of your legs and hips. You use your abs for balance and your arms and shoulders to steer. Because there's resistance, you're strengthening your bones, too. Specially designed bike frames and saddles can make riding safer and easier for various health issues.

7. **Strength Training**

Muscle loss is one of the main reasons people feel less energetic as they get older. When you lift weights, work out on machines, use resistance bands, or do exercises with your own body weight (like push-ups and sit-ups), you build strength, muscle mass, and flexibility. It'll make things like carrying groceries and climbing stairs easier. You can join a gym, but you don't have to. Digging and shoveling in the garden counts, too!

8. **Swimming**

You can exercise for longer in the water than on land. There's no weight putting stress on your joints (and making them hurt), and the water offers resistance to build muscles and bones. Swimming laps burns calories and works your heart like jogging and cycling yet you're not likely to overheat. The moisture helps people with asthma breathe. Water-based exercise improves the mind-set of people with fibromyalgia.

9. Yoga

Actively holding a series of poses will stretch and strengthen your muscles, as well as the tendons and ligaments that hold your bones together. Mindful breathing makes it a kind of meditation, too. Yoga can help lower your heart rate and blood pressure and relieve anxiety and depression. Check out different styles and classes to match your level of fitness and what appeals to you.

10. Moving Meditation- Tai Chi

This quiet exercise is sometimes called "moving meditation." You move your body slowly and gently, flowing from one position to the next, while you breathe deeply. Not only is it good for balance, it can also improve bone and heart health. It may help ease pain and stiffness from arthritis. It might even help you sleep better.

30-day Keto Meal Plan

Day	Breakfast	Lunch	Dinner	Snack/Dessert	Positive hinking Quotes
1	One Pan Peppery Kale Eggs	Cinnamon Spiced Duck in Veggie Broth	Grilled Garlicky Anchovies	Moms Special Deviled Eggs	Life changes very quickly, in a very positive way, if you let it.
2	Cheddar Bacon Omlette	Delicious Chicken Capocollo Bake	Grilled Beef Pecan Salad	Roasted Cauliflower Veggie Bowl	A little progress each day adds up to big results.
3	Cheesy Bacon Muffins with Arugula Salad	Boneless Chicken in Dry Sherry Wine	Mayo Chicken Spanish Pepper Salad	Walnut Brussels Sprouts Bake	Ability is what you're capable of doing. Motivation determines what you do. Attitude determines how well you do it.
4	Buttery Broccoli with Strawberry Lemonade	Oriental Sweets Pepper Turkey Soup	Chicken Lettuce Salad	Garlicky Creamed Spinach	Don't stop until you're proud.
5	Avocado Stacks with Turnip Wedges	Creamy Cheesy Turkey Breast	Pine Nuts and Arugula Salad	Roasted Squash Pumpkin Salad	Eat breakfast like a king, lunch like a prince and dinner like a pauper.
6	Cinnamon Almond Waffles	Chicken Thighs in Coconut Cream	Italian Tomato Avocado Salad	Bulk Italian Sausage Balls	Exercise is king. Nutrition is queen. Put them together and you've got a kingdom.
7	Low Carb Tortilla Salmon Rolls	Dijon Mustard Chicken Mushrooms Skillet	Oregano Spiced Cucumber Salad	Cheesy Bacon with Raw Veggies	Exercise should be regarded as a tribute to the heart.

8	Tofu Kale Wraps	Fennel Bulbs in Chicken Stock	Pepper Roasted Asparagus Salad	Spicy Cheesy Spinach Dip	Fitness is like marriage; you can't cheat on it and expect it to work.
9	Garlicky Spinach Egg Nests	Crispy Bacon and Tender Brussels Sprouts	Citrusy Scallion Chicken Salad	Super Tasty Pecan Coconut Granola Bars	Food can be both enjoyable and nourishing.
10	Buttery Muffins with Tea	Buffalo Mozzarella Cheesed Italian Peppers	Mayo Chicken and Seeds Salad	Sweet and Yummy Pecan Balls	Healthy eating isn't about counting fat grams, dieting, cleanses and antioxidants; it's about eating food untouched from the way we find it in nature in a balanced way.
11	Cheesy Tomato Mushroom Wraps	Spinach Stew with Cold sour cream	Mayo Chicken Spanish Pepper Salad	Choco Chia Pudding	I always believed if you take care of your body it will take care of you.
12	Creamy Cheesy Bacon Cakes	Garlic Spiced Bacon Skillet	Chicken Lettuce Salad	Moms Special Deviled Eggs	I am a better person when I have less on my plate
13	Walnut Cinnamon Muffins	Cheesy Spaghetti Squash Noodles	Pine Nuts and Arugula Salad	Roasted Cauliflower Veggie Bowl	If I don't eat junk, I don't gain weight.
14	Cheesy Zucchini Skillet	Goat Cheesed Zucchini Egg Fritters	Italian Tomato Avocado Salad	Walnut Brussels Sprouts Bake	If it doesn't challenge you, it doesn't change you.
15	Basil Tomato Omelet	One Pan Garlicky Cauliflower Rice	Oregano Spiced Cucumber Salad	Garlicky Creamed Spinach	It has to be hard so you'll never ever forget
16	Walnut Almond Berry Crumble	Baked Turkey with Cauliflower Rice	Pepper Roasted Asparagus Salad	Roasted Squash Pumpkin Salad	It's going to be a journey. It's not a sprint to get in shape.
17	Nuts Sprinkled Zucchini Muffins	Oregano Herbed Cheesy Zucchini	Citrusy Scallion Chicken Salad	Bulk Italian Sausage Balls	Journey of a thousand miles begins with a single step.

18	Creamy Tender Cauliflower	Cayenne Pepper Spiced Creamy Spinach	Mayo Chicken Spanish Pepper Salad	Cheesy Bacon with Raw Veggies	Just believe in yourself. Even if you don't, pretend that you do and, at some point, you will.
19	Cheesy Cauliflower Hash	Chili Spiced Cauliflower Bake	Chicken Lettuce Salad	Spicy Cheesy Spinach Dip	Keep an open mind and a closed refrigerator.
20	Cheesy Egg Skillet	One Pan Cheesy Garlic Kale	Pine Nuts and Arugula Salad	Super Tasty Pecan Coconut Granola Bars	The hard days are what make you stronger.
21	Thyme Herbed Beef and Arugula	Boneless Chicken in Dry Sherry Wine	Italian Tomato Avocado Salad	Sweet and Yummy Pecan Balls	Looking after my health today gives me a better hope for tomorrow.
22	Cheese Biscuits and Pork Gravy	Oriental Sweets Pepper Turkey Soup	Oregano Spiced Cucumber Salad	Choco Chia Pudding	Moderation. Small helpings. Sample a little bit of everything. These are the secrets of happiness and good health.
23	Pork Mixture with Spicy Mayo	Creamy Cheesy Turkey Breast	Pepper Roasted Asparagus Salad	Moms Special Deviled Eggs	My body is less judgmental of my diet than my mind is.
24	Bagel Half with Smoked Salmon	Chicken Thighs in Coconut Cream	Citrusy Scallion Chicken Salad	Roasted Cauliflower Veggie Bowl	New meal; fresh start.
25	Mayo Chicken Salad	Dijon Mustard Chicken Mushrooms Skillet	Mayo Chicken Spanish Pepper Salad	Walnut Brussels Sprouts Bake	Nobody is perfect, so get over the fear of being or doing everything perfectly. Besides, perfect is boring.
26	Low Carb Tomato Soup	Fennel Bulbs in Chicken Stock	Chicken Lettuce Salad	Garlicky Creamed Spinach	Proper nutrition is the difference between feeling exhausted and getting the most out of a workout.
27	Buttery Broccoli with Strawberry Lemonade	Crispy Bacon and Tender Brussels Sprouts	Pine Nuts and Arugula Salad	Roasted Squash Pumpkin Salad	Start where you are. Use what you have. Do what you can.

28	Avocado Stacks with Turnip Wedges	Buffalo Mozzarella Cheesed Italian Peppers	Italian Tomato Avocado Salad	Bulk Italian Sausage Balls	Success is the sum of small efforts, repeated day in and day out.
29	Cinnamon Almond Waffles	Spinach Stew with Cold sour cream	Oregano Spiced Cucumber Salad	Cheesy Bacon with Raw Veggies	Take care of your body. it's the only place you have to live.
30	Low Carb Tortilla Salmon Rolls	Cinnamon Spiced Duck in Veggie Broth	Pepper Roasted Asparagus Salad	Spicy Cheesy Spinach Dip	The groundwork of all happiness is health

Chapter 3: Breakfast and Midday Meals

One Pan Peppery Kale Eggs

Prep time: 7 minutes | Cook time: 13 minutes | Serves 4

- 1 teaspoon butter
- 1 red onion, sliced
- 4 ounce juhs (113 g) chorizo, sliced into thin rounds
- 1 cup chopped kale
- 1 ripe avocado, pitted, peeled, chopped
- 4 eggs
- Salt and black pepper, to season

1. Preheat oven to 370°F (188°C). Melt butter in a cast iron pan over medium heat and sauté the onion for 2 minutes.

2. Add the chorizo and cook for 2 minutes more, flipping once. Introduce the kale in batches with a splash of water to wilt, season lightly with salt, stir and cook for 3 minutes.

3. Mix in the avocado and turn the heat off. Create four holes in the mixture, crack the eggs into each hole, sprinkle with salt and black pepper, and slide the pan into the preheated oven to bake for 6 minutes until the egg whites are set or firm and yolks still runny.

4. Season to taste with salt and pepper, and serve right away with low carb toasts.

Per Serving

Calories: 275 | fat: 23.1g | protein: 12.9g | carbs: 7.7g | net carbs: 4.1g | fiber: 3.6g

Cheddar Bacon Omlette

Prep time: 9 minutes | Cook time: 16 minutes | Serves 4

- 10 slices bacon
- 10 fresh eggs
- 3 tablespoons butter, melted
- ½ cup almond milk
- Salt and black pepper,
- to taste
- 1½ cups Cheddar cheese, shredded
- ¼ cup chopped green onions

1. Preheat the oven to 400°F (205°C) and grease a baking dish with cooking spray.

2. Cook the bacon in a skillet over medium heat for 6 minutes. Once crispy, remove from the skillet to paper towels and discard grease.

3. Chop into small pieces. Whisk the eggs, butter, milk, salt, and black pepper. Mix in the bacon and pour the mixture into the baking dish.

4. Sprinkle with Cheddar cheese and green onions, and bake in the oven for 10 minutes or until the eggs are thoroughly cooked.

5. Remove and cool the frittata for 3 minutes, slice into wedges, and serve warm with a dollop of Greek yogurt.

Per Serving

Calories: 326 | fat: 28.1g | protein: 14.9g | carbs: 2.5g | net carbs: 2.1g | fiber: 0.4g

Cheesy Bacon Muffins with Arugula Salad

Prep time: 10 minutes | Cook time: 20 minutes | Serves 6

- 12 eggs
- ¼ cup coconut milk
- Salt and black pepper, to taste
- 1 cup grated Cheddar cheese
- 12 slices bacon
- 4 jalapeño peppers, seeded and minced

1. Preheat oven to 370°F (188°C). Crack the eggs into a bowl and whisk with coconut milk until combined.
2. Season with salt and pepper, and evenly stir in the Cheddar cheese. Line each hole of a muffin tin with a slice of bacon and fill each with the egg mixture twothirds way up.
3. Top with the jalapeño peppers and bake in the oven for 18 to 20 minutes or until puffed and golden. Remove, allow cooling for a few minutes, and serve with arugula salad.

Per Serving

Calories: 301 | fat: 23.8g | protein: 19.8g | carbs: 3.8g | net carbs: 3.3g | fiber: 0.5g

Buttery Broccoli with Strawberry Lemonade

Prep time: 5 minutes | Cook time: 20 minutes | Serves 4

- 2 heads broccoli, cut into small florets
- 2 red bell peppers, seeded and chopped
- ¼ cup chopped ham
- 2 teaspoons butter
- 1 teaspoon dried oregano plus extra to garnish
- Salt and black pepper, to taste
- 8 fresh eggs

1. Preheat oven to 425°F (220°C). Melt the butter in a frying pan over medium heat; brown the ham, stirring frequently, about 3 minutes.
2. Arrange the broccoli, bell peppers, and ham on a foil-lined baking sheet in a single layer, toss to combine; season with salt, oregano, and black pepper.

3. Bake for 10 minutes until the vegetables have softened. Remove, create eight indentations with a spoon, and crack an egg into each.
4. Return to the oven and continue to bake for an additional 5 to 7 minutes until the egg whites are firm.
5. Season with salt, black pepper, and extra oregano, share the bake into four plates and serve with strawberry lemonade (optional).

Per Serving

Calories: 345 | fat: 27.9g | protein: 11.0g | carbs: 8.9g | net carbs: 4.2g | fiber: 4.7g

Avocado Stacks with Turnip Wedges

Prep time: 5 minutes | Cook time: 15 minutes | Serves 6

- 6 Italian sausage patties
- 4 tablespoons olive oil
- 2 ripe avocados, pitted
- 2 teaspoons fresh lime juice
- Salt and black pepper, to taste
- 6 fresh eggs
- Red pepper flakes, to garnish

1. In a skillet, warm the oil over medium heat and fry the sausage patties about 8 minutes until lightly browned and firm.
2. Remove the patties to a plate. Spoon the avocado into a bowl, mash with the lime juice, and season with salt and black pepper.
3. Spread the mash on the sausages. Boil 3 cups of water in a wide pan over high heat, and reduce to simmer. Crack each egg into a small bowl and gently put the egg into the simmering water; poach for 2 to 3 minutes.
4. Use a perforated spoon to remove from the water on a paper towel to dry. Repeat with the other 5 eggs.
5. Top each stack with a poached egg, sprinkle with chili flakes, salt, black pepper, and chives. Serve with turnip wedges.

Per Serving

Calories: 388 | fat: 22.9g | protein: 16.1g | carbs: 9.6g | net carbs: 5.1g | fiber: 4.5g

Cinnamon Almond Waffles

Prep time: 15 minutes | Cook time: 10 minutes | Serves 6

- 8 ounces (227 g) cream cheese, at room temperature
- 1 teaspoon cinnamon powder
- 3 tablespoons Swerve brown sugar
- Cinnamon powder for garnishing
- 5 tablespoons melted

- butter
- 1½ cups unsweetened almond milk
- 7 large eggs
- ¼ teaspoon liquid stevia
- ½ teaspoon baking powder
- 1½ cups almond flour

1. Combine the cream cheese, cinnamon, and Swerve with a hand mixer until smooth. To make the waffles, whisk the butter, milk, and eggs in a medium bowl.

2. Add the stevia and baking powder and mix. Stir in the almond flour and combine until no lumps exist.

3. Let the batter sit for 5 minutes to thicken. Spritz a waffle iron with a non-stick cooking spray. Ladle a ¼ cup of the batter into the waffle iron and cook until golden, about 10 minutes in total.

4. Repeat with the remaining batter. Slice the waffles into quarters; apply the cinnamon spread in between each of two waffles and snap. Sprinkle with cinnamon powder and serve.

Per Serving

Calories: 308 | fat: 24.1g | protein: 11.9g | carbs: 9.6g | net carbs: 7.8g | fiber: 1.8g

Low Carb Tortilla Salmon Rolls

Prep time: 10 minutes | Cook time: 0 minutes | Serves 3

- 3 tablespoons cream cheese, softened
- 1 small lemon, zested and juiced
- 3 teaspoons chopped fresh dill

- Salt and black pepper, to taste
- 3 (7-inch) low carb tortillas
- 6 slices smoked salmon

1. In a bowl, mix the cream cheese, lemon juice, zest, dill, salt, and black pepper. Lay each tortilla on a plastic wrap (just wide enough to cover the tortilla), spread with cream cheese mixture, and top each (one) with two salmon slices.

2. Roll up the tortillas and secure both ends by twisting. Refrigerate for 2 hours, remove plastic, cut off both ends of each wrap, and cut wraps into wheels.

Per Serving

Calories: 251 | fat: 16.1g | protein: 17.8g | carbs: 8.7g | net carbs: 7.0g | fiber: 1.7g

Tofu Kale Wraps

Prep time: 5 minutes | Cook time: 26 minutes | Serves 4

- 2 tablespoons butter
- 1 cup sliced white mushrooms
- 2 cloves garlic, minced
- 16 ounces (454 g) firm tofu, pressed and

- crumbled
- Salt and black pepper, to taste
- ½ cup thinly sliced kale
- 6 fresh eggs

1. Melt the butter in a non-stick skillet over medium heat, and sauté the mushrooms for 5 minutes until they lose their liquid.

2. Add the garlic and cook for 1 minute. Crumble the tofu into the skillet, season with salt and black pepper. Cook with continuous stirring for 6 minutes. Introduce the kale in batches and cook to soften for about 7 minutes.

3. Crack the eggs into a bowl, whisk until well combined and creamy in color, and pour all over the kale.

4. Use a spatula to immediately stir the eggs while cooking until scrambled and no more runny, about 5 minutes. Plate, and serve with low carb crusted bread.

Per Serving

Calories: 470 | fat: 38.7g | protein: 24.9g | carbs: 7.6g | net carbs: 4.9g | fiber: 2.7g

Garlicky Spinach Egg Nests

Prep time: 13 minutes | Cook time: 22 minutes |

Serves 4

- 2 tablespoons olive oil
- 1 clove garlic, grated
- ½ pound (227 g) spinach, chopped
- Salt and black pepper, to taste
- 2 tablespoons
- shredded Parmesan cheese
- 2 tablespoons shredded gouda cheese
- 4 eggs

1. Preheat oven to 350°F (180°C). Warm the oil in a non-stick skillet over medium heat; add the garlic and sauté until softened for 2 minutes.

2. Add the spinach to wilt for about 5 minutes, and season with salt and black pepper. Allow cooling. Grease a baking sheet with cooking spray, mold 4 (firm and separate) spinach nests on the sheet, and crack an egg into each nest.

3. Sprinkle with Parmesan and gouda cheese. Bake for 15 minutes just until the egg whites have set and the yolks are still runny.

4. Plate the nests and serve right away with low carb toasts and coffee.

Per Serving

Calories: 231 | fat: 17.6g | protein: 12.2g | carbs: 5.4g | net carbs: 4.1g | fiber: 1.3g

Buttery Muffins with Tea

Prep time: 10 minutes | Cook time: 20 minutes | Serves 4

- 2 drops liquid stevia
- 2 cups almond flour
- 2 teaspoons baking powder
- ½ teaspoon salt
- 8 ounces (227 g) cream
- cheese, softened
- ¼ cup melted butter
- 1 egg
- 1 cup unsweetened almond milk

1. Preheat oven to 400°F (205°C) and grease a 12-cup muffin tray with cooking spray. Mix the flour, baking powder, and salt in a large bowl.

2. In a separate bowl, beat the cream cheese, stevia, and butter using a hand mixer and whisk in the egg and milk. Fold in the flour, and spoon the batter into the muffin cups two-thirds way up.

3. Bake for 20 minutes until puffy at the top and

golden brown, remove to a wire rack to cool slightly for 5 minutes before serving. Serve with tea.

Per Serving

Calories: 321 | fat: 30.5g | protein: 4.1g | carbs: 8.1g | net carbs: 5.9g | fiber: 2.2g

Cheesy Tomato Mushroom Wraps

Prep time: 10 minutes | Cook time: 10 minutes | Serves 4

- 6 eggs
- 2 tablespoons almond milk
- 1 tablespoon olive oil
- Sea salt, to taste
- 1 teaspoon olive oil
- 1 cup mushrooms, chopped
- Salt and black pepper, to taste
- ½ teaspoon cayenne pepper
- 8 fresh lettuce leaves
- 4 slices Gruyere cheese
- 2 tomatoes, sliced

1. Mix all the ingredients for the wraps thoroughly. Set a frying pan over medium heat. Add in ¼ of the mixture and cook for 4 minutes on both sides.

2. Do the same thrice and set the wraps aside, they should be kept warm. In a separate pan over medium heat, warm 1 teaspoon of olive oil.

3. Cook the mushrooms for 5 minutes until soft; add cayenne pepper, black pepper, and salt.

4. Set 1-2 lettuce leaves onto every wrap, split the mushrooms among the wraps and top with tomatoes and cheese.

Per Serving

Calories: 471 | fat: 43.9g | protein: 19.4g | carbs: 6.5g | net carbs: 5.3g | fiber: 1.2g

Creamy Cheesy Bacon Cakes

Prep time: 6 minutes | Cook time: 2 minutes | Serves 2

- ¼ cup flax meal
- 1 egg
- 2 tablespoons heavy cream
- 2 tablespoons pesto
- ¼ cup almond flour
- ¼ teaspoon baking soda

- Salt and black pepper, to taste
- 2 tablespoons cream cheese
- 4 slices bacon
- ½ medium avocado, sliced

1. Mix together the dry muffin ingredients in a bowl. Add egg, heavy cream, and pesto, and whisk well with a fork.
2. Season with salt and pepper. Divide the mixture between two ramekins. Place in the microwave and cook for 60-90 seconds.
3. Leave to cool slightly before filling. Meanwhile, in a skillet, over medium heat, cook the bacon slices until crispy.
4. Transfer to paper towels to soak up excess fat; set aside. Invert the muffins onto a plate and cut in half, crosswise.
5. To assemble the sandwiches: spread cream cheese and top with bacon and avocado slices.

Per Serving

Calories: 512 | fat: 38.3g | protein: 16.3g | carbs: 10.3g | net carbs: 4.4g | fiber: 5.9g

Walnut Cinnamon Muffins

Prep time: 5 minutes | Cook time: 15 minutes | Serves 6

- ¾ cup mascarpone cheese
- ¼ cup natural yogurt
- 3 eggs, beaten
- 1 tablespoon walnuts, ground
- 4 tablespoons erythritol
- ½ teaspoon vanilla essence
- ⅓ teaspoon ground cinnamon

1. Set oven to 360°F (182°C) and grease a muffin pan. Mix all ingredients in a bowl. Split the batter into the muffin cups.
2. Bake for 12 to 15 minutes. Remove and set on a wire rack to cool slightly before serving.

Per Serving

Calories: 182 | fat: 13.6g | protein: 10.4g | carbs: 3.8g | net carbs: 3.6g | fiber: 0.2g

Cheesy Zucchini Skillet

Prep time: 20 minutes | Cook time: 10 minutes |

Serves 6

- 4 cups zucchini, spiralized
- ½ pound (227 g) bacon, chopped
- 6 ounces (170 g) cottage cheese, curds
- 6 ounces (170 g) cream cheese
- 1 cup Fontina cheese
- ½ cup dill pickles, chopped, squeezed
- 2 cloves garlic, crushed
- 1 cup grated Parmesan cheese
- ½ teaspoon caraway seeds
- ¼ teaspoon dried dill weed
- ½ teaspoon onion powder
- Salt and black pepper, to taste
- 1 cup crushed pork rinds
- Cooking oil

1. Thoroughly mix zoodles, cottage cheese, dill pickles, ½ cup of Parmesan cheese, garlic, cream cheese, bacon, and Fontina cheese until well combined.
2. Shape the mixture into balls. Refrigerate for 3 hours. In a mixing bowl, mix the remaining ½ cup of Parmesan cheese, crushed pork rinds, dill, black pepper, onion powder, caraway seeds, and salt.
3. Roll cheese ball in Parmesan mixture to coat. Set a skillet over medium heat and warm 1-inch of oil.
4. Fry cheese balls until browned on all sides. Set on a paper towel to soak up any excess oil.

Per Serving

Calories: 406 | fat: 26.7g | protein: 33.3g | carbs: 8.6g | net carbs: 5.7g | fiber: 2.9g

Basil Tomato Omelet

Prep time: 8 minutes | Cook time: 7 minutes | Serves 1

- 2 eggs
- 6 basil leaves
- 2 ounces (57 g) Mozzarella cheese
- 1 tablespoon butter
- 1 tablespoon water
- 4 thin slices chorizo
- 1 tomato, sliced
- Salt and black pepper, to taste

1. Whisk the eggs along with the water and some salt and pepper. Melt the butter in a skillet and cook the eggs for 30 seconds.
2. Spread the chorizo slices over. Arrange the tomato

and Mozzarella over the chorizo. Cook for about 3 minutes.

3. Cover the skillet and cook for 3 minutes until omelet is set. When ready, remove the pan from heat; run a spatula around the edges of the omelet and flip it onto a warm plate, folded side down.

4. Serve garnished with basil leaves and green salad.

Per Serving

Calories: 452 | fat: 36.4g | protein: 30.1g | carbs: 5.4g | net carbs: 2.9g | fiber: 2.5g

Walnut Almond Berry Crumble

Prep time: 10 minutes | Cook time: 25 minutes | Serves 4

- 6 tablespoons cold unsalted butter, divided
- ¼ cup almond flour
- ¼ cup ground flaxseed
- ¼ cup slivered almonds
- ¼ cup chopped roasted unsalted walnuts
- 1 cup fresh or frozen blueberries

- 2 to 4 tablespoons granulated sugar-free sweetener
- Zest of 1 lemon
- 1 teaspoon vanilla extract
- ½ teaspoon ground ginger or cinnamon
- ½ cup heavy cream
- 2 cups plain full-fat Greek yogurt

1. Preheat the oven to 350°F (177°C) and generously coat the bottom and sides of an 8-inch square glass baking dish or 8-inch pie pan with 2 tablespoons of butter.

2. In a medium bowl, cut the remaining 4 tablespoons of butter into very small pieces. Add the almond flour, flaxseed, almonds, and walnuts and mix until crumbly. Set aside.

3. In a separate bowl, combine the blueberries, sweetener, lemon zest, vanilla extract, and ginger or cinnamon. Toss to coat the blueberries well.

4. Add the blueberry mixture to the prepared baking dish (they won't quite cover the bottom), and pour the heavy cream over the blueberry mixture.

5. Top the blueberry mixture evenly with the flour-and-nut mixture, and bake for 20 to 25 minutes,

until golden brown. Let rest for 10 minutes before serving to allow the mixture to thicken.

6. To serve, top one-quarter of the warm crumble mixture with ½ cup of Greek yogurt.

Per Serving

Calories: 500 | fat: 45g | protein: 10g | carbs: 18g | net carbs: 13g | fiber: 5g

Nuts Sprinkled Zucchini Muffins

Prep time: 10 minutes | Cook time: 20 minutes | Serves 12

- Butter or coconut oil, for greasing (optional)
- 1½ cups shredded zucchini (1 large or 2 small zucchini)
- 1 teaspoon salt
- 2 large eggs
- ⅓ cup granulated sugar-free sweetener of choice (monk fruit, stevia, etc.)
- ¼ cup extra-virgin olive oil (or melted coconut oil)

- 1¾ cups almond flour
- ¼ cup ground flaxseed or flax meal
- 1 teaspoon baking soda
- ½ teaspoon ground cinnamon
- ½ teaspoon ground ginger (optional)
- ½ cup chopped walnuts or pecans, plus 2 tablespoons finely chopped nuts

1. Preheat the oven to 350°F (177°C). Line a 12-muffin tin with liners or coat well with butter or coconut oil.

2. Drain the zucchini: Place the shredded zucchini in a colander or on several layers of paper towels.

3. Sprinkle with the salt and let sit for 10 minutes. Using another paper towel, press on the zucchini to release any excess moisture.

4. In a large bowl, whisk together the eggs, granulated sweetener, and olive oil. Add the zucchini, almond flour, flaxseed, baking soda, cinnamon, and ginger and mix until well incorporated. Stir in ½ cup of chopped nuts.

5. Divide the batter evenly between the 12 prepared muffin cups, filling each about three-quarters full. Sprinkle 2 tablespoons of finely chopped nuts evenly among the 12 filled muffin tins.

6. Bake until a toothpick inserted in the center of a muffin comes out clean, 15 to 18 minutes.

Per Serving

Calories: 170 | fat: 16g | protein: 5g | carbs: 4g | net carbs: 2g | fiber: 2g

Creamy Tender Cauliflower

Prep time: 5 minutes | Cook time: 15 minutes | Serves 4

- ¼ cup heavy cream
- 4 tablespoons unsalted butter, divided
- 1 teaspoon salt
- ½ teaspoon garlic powder
- ¼ teaspoon freshly
- ground black pepper
- 2 cups riced cauliflower
- ¾ cup shredded cheddar cheese
- ¼ cup shredded Parmesan cheese

1. In a medium saucepan over high heat, combine the heavy cream, 2 tablespoons of butter, salt, garlic powder, and pepper and bring to just below a boil. Add the rice cauliflower and reduce heat to low.

2. Simmer, stirring occasionally, for 8 to 10 minutes, until the cauliflower is tender, most of the water from the vegetable has evaporated, and the mixture is thick and creamy.

3. Remove from the heat and stir in the shredded cheeses and remaining 2 tablespoons of butter. Serve warm.

Per Serving

Calories: 280 | fat: 16g | protein: 8g | carbs: 5g | net carbs: 4g | fiber: 1g

Cheesy Cauliflower Hash

Prep time: 10 minutes | Cook time: 20 minutes | Serves 4

- 2 cups riced cauliflower, fresh or frozen
- 2 ounces cream cheese, room temperature
- 2 tablespoons ground flaxseed or flax meal
- 2 tablespoons almond flour
- ½ teaspoon garlic powder
- 1 teaspoon baking powder
- 1 teaspoon salt, divided
- 1 large egg, lightly beaten
- 2 tablespoons minced scallions, green and white parts
- 6 tablespoons extra-virgin olive oil, divided
- 1 small very ripe avocado, peeled, pitted, and mashed
- 1 teaspoon white wine vinegar or lemon juice
- ¼ teaspoon freshly ground black pepper

1. Steam or microwave the riced cauliflower, covered, until tender. For frozen, cook 2 to 3 minutes in the microwave or 4 to 5 minutes on the stovetop. For fresh, cook 1 to 2 minutes in the microwave or 3 to 4 minutes on the stovetop. Set aside until completely cooled.

2. Meanwhile, in a medium bowl, mix the cream cheese until smooth. Add the flaxseed, almond flour, garlic powder, baking powder, ½ teaspoon of salt, and the beaten egg and whisk to combine well.

3. When the cauliflower reaches room temperature, cover with a paper towel. Use your hands to press down, allowing the liquid to rise above the towel, and pour off the excess. Continue pressing until the cauliflower is mostly dried and drained of excess liquid.

4. Stir the cauliflower and scallions into the cream cheese mixture.

5. Heat 2 tablespoons of olive oil in a large skillet over medium heat. Drop heaping table spoon full of the cauliflower batter onto the skillet, and press down with a spatula to form 4 to 6 small patties, depending on the size of the skillet.

6. Cook for 2 to 4 minutes, until the bottom is browned, then flip and cook another 2 to 4 minutes. Repeat with another 2 tablespoons of olive oil and the remaining batter.

7. To prepare the avocado mayo, in a small bowl, blend the remaining 2 tablespoons of olive oil, the mashed avocado, the remaining ½ teaspoon of salt, the vinegar or lemon juice, and pepper and whisk or beat with a fork until smooth and creamy.

8. Serve the hash browns warm with avocado mayo.

Per Serving

Calories: 379 | fat: 37g | protein: 6g | carbs: 10g | net carbs: 4g | fiber: 6g

Cheesy Egg Skillet

Prep time: 2 minutes | Cook time: 3 minutes | Serves 2

- 4 large eggs
- ½ teaspoon salt
- ¼ teaspoon freshly ground black pepper
- 2 tablespoons unsalted butter
- ¼ cup Bacon-Studded Pimento Cheese

1. In a small bowl, whisk together the eggs, salt, and pepper. Set aside.

2. Melt the butter in a small skillet over medium heat. Add the whisked eggs and reduce heat to low. Stirring constantly with a spatula, scramble the eggs for 1 to 2 minutes, until no longer runny, but not fully cooked through.

3. Remove the skillet from the heat and stir in the pimento cheese for an additional 30 seconds, or until melted and well combined.

Per Serving

Calories: 353 | fat: 31g | protein: 17g | carbs: 2g | net carbs: 2g | fiber: 0g

Thyme Herbed Beef and Arugula

Prep time: 10 minutes | Cook time: 10 minutes | Serves 2

- 2 tablespoons unsalted butter
- 1 tablespoon almond flour
- 1 ounce cream cheese, room temperature
- ½ teaspoon dried thyme or other herb such as rosemary, oregano, or sage
- ¼ teaspoon freshly ground black pepper
- ½ cup heavy cream
- 8 ounces cooked steak, cut into very thin strips, or deli roast beef (see ingredient tip)
- 2 cups baby arugula (or chopped fresh baby spinach leaves)
- 1 Microwave Keto Bread round, halved and toasted

1. Melt the butter in a medium saucepan over low heat. Add the almond flour and whisk for 1

minute, until slightly browned.

2. Add the cream cheese, thyme, and pepper, and whisk until the cheese is melted, 1 to 2 minutes.

3. Increase heat to medium-high. Whisking constantly, stream in the cream and continue whisking until thickened, 3 to 4 minutes. Add the sliced steak and arugula, reduce heat to low, and stir to combine. Cook for another 1 to 2 minutes or until the beef is heated through and the arugula is wilted.

4. To serve, top each toasted sandwich round half with half of the beef and arugula mixture.

Per Serving

Calories: 703 | fat: 59g | protein: 38g | carbs: 5g | net carbs: 4g | fiber: 1g

Cheese Biscuits and Pork Gravy

Prep time: 10 minutes | Cook time: 13 minutes | Serves 4

For the Biscuit:

- 1 cup almond flour
- 1½ teaspoons baking powder
- ½ teaspoon salt
- 2 tablespoons cold unsalted butter, diced
- 2 tablespoons heavy cream
- ½ cup shredded mozzarella or cheddar cheese
- 1 large egg

For the Gravy:

- 8 ounces ground Italian pork sausage (not sweet)
- 4 ounces cream cheese, room temperature
- ½ cup heavy cream
- ½ cup chicken or beef bone broth
- 1 teaspoon onion powder
- 1 teaspoon salt
- ¼ teaspoon freshly ground black pepper

1. To make the biscuits. Preheat the oven to 375°F and line a large baking sheet with parchment paper.

2. In a large bowl, combine the almond flour, baking powder, and salt and mix well. Add the butter, and use a fork to crumble into the flour mixture until it resembles coarse pebbles.

3. Use the fork to whisk in the heavy cream, 1

tablespoon at a time. Whisk in the cheese and egg until a smooth dough forms.

4. Cut the dough into four equal pieces and form each into a ball. Place on the prepared baking sheet, pressing down slightly with the heel of your palm to flatten a bit, and bake for 16 to 18 minutes, or until golden brown.

5. To make the gravy. While the biscuits bake, brown the sausage in a medium saucepan over medium heat until cooked through, 3 to 4 minutes. Do not drain the rendered fat.

6. Add the cream cheese, heavy cream, bone broth, onion powder, salt, and pepper to the sausage and reduce heat to low. Stirring constantly, simmer until thickened, another 6 to 8 minutes.

7. Halve the biscuits horizontally and serve topped with gravy.

Per Serving

Calories: 674 | fat: 63g | protein: 20g | carbs: 9g | net carbs: 6g | fiber: 3g

Pork Mixture with Spicy Mayo

Prep time: 10 minutes | Cook time: 10 minutes | Serves 2

- 2 large eggs
- 2 tablespoons sesame oil, divided
- 2 tablespoons soy sauce, divided
- 2 tablespoons extra-virgin olive oil
- 6 ounces ground pork
- 1 tablespoon chopped fresh ginger (or 1 teaspoon ground ginger)
- 2 cloves garlic, minced
- 2 cups finely chopped cabbage

- 2 ribs celery, diced
- ½ small red bell pepper, diced
- 2 tablespoons lime juice, divided
- 2 scallions, minced (green and white parts)
- 2 tablespoons mayonnaise
- 1 teaspoon sriracha or other hot sauce
- ½ teaspoon garlic powder

1. In a small bowl, beat together the eggs, 1 tablespoon of sesame oil, and 1 tablespoon of soy sauce and set aside.

2. Heat the olive oil in a large skillet over medium heat. Sauté the ground pork, breaking it apart, until browned and no longer pink, 4 to 5 minutes. Add the ginger and garlic and sauté for an additional 30 seconds.

3. Add the cabbage, celery, and bell pepper and sauté, stirring constantly, until the vegetables are wilted and fragrant, another 2 to 3 minutes.

4. Push the vegetables and pork to one side of the skillet and add the egg mixture to the other side. Reduce heat to low and scramble the egg until cooked through, 1 to 2 minutes. Remove the skillet from the heat and mix the egg into the pork and cabbage.

5. In a small bowl, whisk together the remaining 1 tablespoon of sesame oil, the remaining 1 tablespoon of soy sauce, 1 tablespoon of lime juice, and the scallions. Pour over the cooked pork mixture and stir to combine well, reserving the bowl.

6. In the same small bowl, combine the remaining 1 tablespoon of lime juice, the mayonnaise, sriracha, and garlic powder.

7. Divide the pork mixture evenly between two bowls and drizzle each with half of the spicy mayo. Serve warm.

Per Serving

Calories: 695 | fat: 61g | protein: 25g | carbs: 14g | net carbs: 10g | fiber: 4g

Bagel Half with Smoked Salmon

Prep time: 10 minutes | Cook time: 20 minutes | Serves 6

- 8 ounces cream cheese, room temperature, divided
- 2½ cups shredded mozzarella or Swiss cheese (not cheddar)
- 1½ cups almond flour
- 1 tablespoon baking powder
- 2 large eggs, beaten

- 1 tablespoon sesame seeds
- 1 tablespoon poppy seeds
- 1 tablespoon whole flaxseed or chia seeds
- ¼ cup extra-virgin olive oil
- 2 tablespoons chopped capers

(optional)
- 6 ounces smoked salmon
- 2 tablespoons very thinly sliced red onion

1. Preheat the oven to 400°F and line a baking sheet with parchment paper.

2. Place 2 ounces of cream cheese in a medium microwave-safe bowl and mash well with a fork. Add the shredded cheese and stir to combine. Microwave on high for 1½ minutes, or until the cheeses start to melt. Stir well and microwave on high for an additional 30 to 90 seconds, or until well melted and smooth when stirred.

3. While the cheese melts, combine the almond flour and baking powder in a large bowl, breaking up any lumps. Whisk in the beaten eggs.

4. Add the melted cheese mixture to the almond flour mixture and knead the dough with your hands for 3 to 4 minutes or until the cheese is well incorporated into the flour. The dough will be very sticky.

5. In a small bowl, mix together the sesame seeds, poppy seeds, and flaxseed. Set aside.

6. Divide the dough into six even balls and roll each out to a 6-inch log. Curve the log to form a circle, pressing the ends together to seal. Dip the front of each bagel into the bowl of seeds, pressing so they stick. Place each bagel 4 inches apart on the prepared baking sheet.

7. Bake for 12 to 15 minutes, or until golden brown. Remove from the oven, transfer to a cooling rack, and allow to cool to the touch.

8. To assemble the lox, slice three bagels in half (reserving the other three for another use). In a small bowl, combine the remaining 6 tablespoons of cream cheese, the olive oil, and capers (if using) and whisk until smooth.

9. Top each bagel half with 2 tablespoons of cream cheese mixture, 1 ounce of smoked salmon, and a few slivered red onions.

Per Serving

Calories: 575 | fat: 49g | protein: 26g | carbs: 11g | net carbs: 7g | fiber: 4g

Mayo Chicken Salad

Prep time: 10 minutes | Cook time: 0 minutes | Serves 4

- ½ cup mayonnaise
- 1 tablespoon Dijon mustard
- 1 teaspoon salt
- ½ to 1 teaspoon dried tarragon or other herb such as rosemary, oregano, or thyme (optional)
- ¼ teaspoon freshly ground black pepper
- 2 cups chopped cooked chicken thighs (or pulled rotisserie chicken)
- 2 ribs celery, chopped
- ½ small Granny Smith apple, cored and seeded, diced
- ½ cup chopped walnuts or pecans

1. In a medium bowl, combine the mayonnaise, mustard, salt, tarragon (if using), and pepper.

2. Add the chopped chicken to the mayonnaise mixture. Add the celery, apple, and walnuts and stir to combine well.

3. Store leftovers covered in the refrigerator for up to 3 days.

Per Serving

Calories: 435 | fat: 37g | protein: 20g | carbs: 5g | net carbs: 3g | fiber: 2g

Low Carb Tomato Soup

Prep time: 10 minutes | Cook time: 40 minutes | Serves 4

- 4 medium whole tomatoes, cored
- 8 medium garlic cloves, peeled
- ½ medium yellow onion, quartered
- ¼ cup extra-virgin olive oil, divided
- 2 tablespoons fresh rosemary (or 2 teaspoons dried)
- 1 teaspoon salt, plus
- more
- 1 cup chicken or vegetable stock
- 1 cup heavy cream, divided
- 1 cup fresh basil, roughly chopped
- 1 tablespoon balsamic or red wine vinegar
- ¼ to ½ teaspoon red pepper flakes

1. Preheat the oven to 400°F (204°C).

2. In a bowl, combine the tomatoes, garlic cloves, onion quarters, 2 tablespoons of olive oil, the rosemary, and salt. Toss to coat the vegetables

with the oil. Transfer to an 8-inch square glass baking dish, cover with aluminum foil, and roast until the tomatoes have released most of their juices, 30 to 35 minutes. Allow to cool for 10 minutes.

3. Transfer the contents of the baking dish, including the liquids, to a blender, or transfer to a large bowl and use an immersion or stick blender. Add the stock, the remaining 2 tablespoons of olive oil, ¾ cup of the cream, the basil, vinegar, and red pepper flakes and blend until smooth and creamy.

4. Transfer the mixture to a medium saucepan and heat over medium-low heat, stirring constantly, until heated through. Season to taste with additional salt if desired and serve warm, drizzled with the remaining cream.

Per Serving

Calories: 364 | fat: 36g | protein: 3g | carbs: 10g | net carbs: 8g | fiber: 2g

Chapter 4: Vegetable Mains

White Cabbage in Cream of Celery

Prep time: 8 minutes | Cook time: 22 minutes | Serves 3

- 6 ounces (170 g) Goan chorizo sausage, sliced
- 2 cloves garlic, finely chopped
- 1 teaspoon Indian spice blend
- 1 pound (454 g) white cabbage, outer leaves removed and finely shredded
- ¾ cup cream of celery soup

1. Heat a large-sized wok over a moderate flame. Now, sear the Goan chorizo sausage until no longer pink; reserve.

2. Cook the garlic and Indian spice blend in the pan drippings until they are aromatic. Now, stir in the cabbage and cream of celery soup.

3. Turn the temperature to medium-low, cover, and continue simmering an additional 22 minutes or until tender and heated through.

4. Add the reserved Goan chorizo sausage; ladle into individual bowls and serve. Enjoy!

Per Serving

Calories: 236 | fat: 17.7g | protein: 9.8g | carbs: 6.1g | net carbs: 3.7g | fiber: 2.4g

Cheesy Brown Cauliflower

Prep time: 5 minutes | Cook time: 25 minutes | Serves 6

- 1½ pounds (680 g) cauliflower, broken into small florets
- ½ cup Greek yogurt
- 4 eggs, beaten
- 6 ounces (170 g) ham, diced
- 1 cup Swiss cheese, preferably freshly grated

1. Place the cauliflower into a deep saucepan; cover with water and bring to a boil over high heat; immediately reduce the heat to medium-low.

2. Let it simmer, covered, approximately 6 minutes. Drain and mash with a potato masher. Add in the yogurt, eggs and ham; stir until everything is well combined and incorporated.

3. Scrape the mixture into a lightly greased casserole dish.

4. Top with the grated Swiss cheese and transfer to a preheated at 390°F (199°C) oven.

5. Bake for 15 to 20 minutes or until cheese bubbles and browns.

Per Serving

Calories: 237 | fat: 13.6g | protein: 20.2g | carbs: 7.1g | net carbs: 4.8g | fiber: 2.3g

One Pan Cheesy Garlic Kale

Prep time: 5 minutes | Cook time: 10 minutes | Serves 3

- ½ tablespoon olive oil
- 1 teaspoon fresh garlic, chopped
- 9 ounces (255 g) kale,
- torn into pieces
- ½ cup Cottage cheese, creamed
- ½ teaspoon sea salt

1. Heat the olive oil in a saucepan over a moderate flame. Now, cook the garlic until just tender and aromatic.

2. Then, stir in the kale and continue to cook for about 10 minutes until all liquid evaporates.

3. Fold in the Cottage cheese and salt; stir until everything is heated through. Enjoy!

Per Serving

Calories: 94 | fat: 4.5g | protein: 7.0g | carbs: 6.2g | net carbs: 3.5g | fiber: 2.7g

Chili Spiced Cauliflower Bake

Prep time: 20 minutes | Cook time: 20 minutes | Serves 4

- ½ teaspoon butter, melted
- 1 (½-pound / 227-g) head cauliflower, broken into florets
- ½ cup Swiss cheese, shredded
- ½ cup Mexican blend cheese, room temperature
- ½ cup Greek yogurt
- 1 cup cooked ham, chopped
- 1 roasted chili pepper, chopped
- ½ teaspoon porcini powder
- 1 teaspoon garlic powder
- 1 teaspoon shallot powder
- ½ teaspoon cayenne pepper
- ¼ teaspoon dried sage
- ½ teaspoon dried oregano
- Sea salt and ground black pepper, to taste

1. Preheat the oven to 340°F (171°C). Coat the bottom and sides of a casserole dish with ½ teaspoon of melted butter.

2. Empty the cauliflower into a pot and cover it with water. Let it cook for 6 minutes until it is tender.

3. Mash the cauliflower with a potato masher. Stir in the cheese until the cheese has melted.

4. Add Greek yogurt, chopped ham, roasted pepper, and spices. Place the mixture in the prepared casserole dish; bake for 20 minutes.

5. Let it sit for about 10 minutes before cutting. Serve.

Per Serving

Calories: 189 | fat: 11.3g | protein: 14.9g | carbs: 5.7g | net carbs: 4.6g | fiber: 1.1g

Cayenne Pepper Spiced Creamy Spinach

Prep time: 5 minutes | Cook time: 5 minutes | Serves 4

- 1 tablespoon butter, room temperature
- 1 clove garlic, minced
- 10 ounces (283 g) spinach
- ½ teaspoon garlic salt
- ¼ teaspoon ground
- black pepper, or more to taste
- ½ teaspoon cayenne pepper
- 3 ounces (85 g) cream cheese
- ½ cup double cream

1. Melt the butter in a saucepan that is preheated over medium heat. Once hot. Cook garlic for 30 seconds.

2. Now, add the spinach; cover the pan for 2 minutes to let the spinach wilt. Season with salt, black pepper, and cayenne pepper.

3. Stir in cheese and cream; stir until the cheese melts. Serve immediately.

Per Serving

Calories: 167 | fat: 15.1g | protein: 4.4g | carbs: 5.0g | net carbs: 3.3g | fiber: 1.7g

Oregano Herbed Cheesy Zucchini

Prep time: 15 minutes | Cook time: 45 minutes | Serves 4

- Nonstick cooking spray
- 2 cups zucchini, thinly sliced
- 2 tablespoons leeks, sliced
- ½ teaspoon salt
- Freshly ground black pepper, to taste
- ½ teaspoon dried basil
- ½ teaspoon dried
- oregano
- ½ cup Cheddar cheese, grated
- ¼ cup heavy cream
- 4 tablespoons Parmesan cheese, freshly grated
- 1 tablespoon butter, room temperature
- 1 teaspoon fresh garlic, minced

1. Start by preheating your oven to 370°F (188°C). Lightly grease a casserole dish with a nonstick

cooking spray. Place 1 cup of the zucchini slices in the dish; add 1 tablespoon of leeks; sprinkle with salt, pepper, basil, and oregano.

2. Top with ¼ cup of Cheddar cheese. Repeat the layers one more time. In a mixing dish, thoroughly whisk the heavy cream with Parmesan, butter, and garlic. Spread this mixture over the zucchini layer and cheese layers.

3. Place in the preheated oven and bake for about 40 to 45 minutes until the edges are nicely browned. Sprinkle with chopped chives, if desired.

Per Serving

Calories: 156 | fat: 12.8g | protein: 7.5g | carbs: 3.6g | net carbs: 2.8g | fiber: 0.8g

Baked Turkey with Cauliflower Rice

Prep time: 15 minutes | Cook time: 45 minutes | Serves 6

- 2 tablespoons vegetable oil
- 2 tablespoons yellow onion, chopped
- 1 teaspoon fresh garlic, crushed
- ½ pound (227 g) ground pork
- ½ pound (227 g) ground turkey
- 1 cup cauliflower rice
- ½ teaspoon sea salt
- ¼ teaspoon red pepper flakes, crushed
- ½ teaspoon ground black pepper
- 1 teaspoon dried parsley flakes
- 6 medium-sized bell peppers, seeded and cleaned
- ½ cup tomato sauce
- ½ cup Cheddar cheese, shredded

1. Heat the oil in a pan over medium flame. Once hot, sauté the onion and garlic for 2 to 3 minutes.

2. Add the ground meat and cook for 6 minutes longer or until it is nicely browned. Add cauliflower rice and seasoning.

3. Continue to cook for a further 3 minutes. Divide the filling between the prepared bell peppers. Cover with a piece of foil.

4. Place the peppers in a baking pan; add tomato sauce. Bake in the preheated oven at 380°F (193°C) for 20 minutes.

5. Uncover, top with cheese, and bake for 10 minutes

more. Bon appétit!

Per Serving

Calories: 245 | fat: 12.8g | protein: 16.6g | carbs: 3.3g | net carbs: 2.3g | fiber: 1.0g

One Pan Garlicky Cauliflower Rice

Prep time: 7 minutes | Cook time: 8 minutes | Serves 3

- ½ pound (227 g) fresh cauliflower
- 1 tablespoon sesame oil
- ½ cup leeks, chopped
- 1 garlic, pressed
- Sea salt and freshly ground black pepper, to taste
- ½ teaspoon Chinese five-spice powder
- 1 teaspoon oyster sauce
- ½ teaspoon light soy sauce
- 1 tablespoon Shaoxing wine
- 3 eggs

1. Pulse the cauliflower in a food processor until it resembles rice. Heat the sesame oil in a pan over medium-high heat; sauté the leeks and garlic for 2 to 3 minutes.

2. Add the prepared cauliflower rice to the pan, along with salt, black pepper, and Chinese five-spice powder.

3. Next, add oyster sauce, soy sauce, and wine. Let it cook, stirring occasionally, until the cauliflower is crisp-tender, about 5 minutes.

4. Then, add the eggs to the pan; stir until everything is well combined. Serve warm and enjoy!

Per Serving

Calories: 132 | fat: 8.8g | protein: 7.2g | carbs: 6.2g | net carbs: 4.4g | fiber: 1.8g

Goat Cheesed Zucchini Egg Fritters

Prep time: 10 minutes | Cook time: 5 minutes | Serves 6

- 1 pound (454 g) zucchini, grated and drained
- 1 egg
- 1 teaspoon fresh Italian parsley

- ½ cup almond meal
- ½ cup goat cheese, crumbled
- Sea salt and ground
- black pepper, to taste
- ½ teaspoon red pepper flakes, crushed
- 2 tablespoons olive oil

1. Mix all ingredients, except for the olive oil, in a large bowl. Let it sit in your refrigerator for 30 minutes.
2. Heat the oil in a non-stick frying pan over medium heat; scoop the heaped tablespoons of the zucchini mixture into the hot oil.
3. Cook for 3 to 4 minutes; then, gently flip the fritters over and cook on the other side.
4. Cook in a couple of batches. Transfer to a paper towel to soak up any excess grease. Serve and enjoy!

Per Serving

Calories: 110 | fat: 8.8g | protein: 5.8g | carbs: 3.2g | net carbs: 2.2g | fiber: 1.0g

Cheesy Spaghetti Squash Noodles

Prep time: 15 minutes | Cook time: 50 to 60 minutes | Serves 4

- ½ pound (227 g) spaghetti squash, halved, scoop out seeds
- 1 teaspoon olive oil
- ½ cup Mozzarella cheese, shredded
- ½ cup cream cheese
- ½ cup full-fat Greek
- yogurt
- 2 eggs
- 1 garlic clove, minced
- ½ teaspoon cumin
- ½ teaspoon basil ½ teaspoon mint
- Sea salt and ground black pepper, to taste

1. Place the squash halves in a baking pan; drizzle the insides of each squash half with olive oil.
2. Bake in the preheated oven at 370°F (188°C) for 45 to 50 minutes or until the interiors are easily pierced through with a fork.
3. Now, scrape out the spaghetti squash "noodles" from the skin in a mixing bowl. Add the remaining ingredients and mix to combine well. Carefully fill each of the squash half with the cheese mixture.
4. Bake at 350°F (180°C) for 5 to 10 minutes, until the

cheese is bubbling and golden brown.

Per Serving

Calories: 220 | fat: 17.6g | protein: 9.0g | carbs: 6.8g | net carbs: 5.9g | fiber: 0.9g

Garlic Spiced Bacon Skillet

Prep time: 10 minutes | Cook time: 15 minutes | Serves 3

- 4 ounces (113 g) bacon, diced
- 1 medium-sized onion, chopped
- 2 cloves garlic, minced
- ½ teaspoon caraway seeds
- 1 bay laurel
- ½ teaspoon cayenne pepper
- 1 pound (454 g) red cabbage, shredded
- ¼ teaspoon ground black pepper, to season
- 1 cup beef bone broth

1. Heat up a nonstick skillet over a moderate flame. Cook the bacon for 3 to 4 minutes, stirring continuously; set aside.
2. In the same skillet, sauté the onion for 2 to 3 minutes or until it has softened. Now, sauté the garlic and caraway seeds for 30 seconds more or until aromatic.
3. Then, add in the remaining ingredients and stir to combine. Reduce the temperature to medium-low, cover, and cook for 10 minutes longer; stirring periodically to ensure even cooking.
4. Serve in individual bowls, garnished with the reserved bacon. Enjoy!

Per Serving

Calories: 242 | fat: 22.2g | protein: 6.5g | carbs: 6.8g | net carbs: 4.9g | fiber: 1.9g

Spinach Stew with Cold sour cream

Prep time: 10 minutes | Cook time: 30 minutes | Serves 4

- 2 tablespoons olive oil
- 1 Spanish onion, peeled and diced
- 1 garlic clove, minced
- ½ pound (227 g) butternut squash, diced
- 1 celery stalk, chopped

- 3 cups vegetable broth
- Kosher salt and freshly cracked black pepper, to taste
- 4 cups baby spinach
- 4 tablespoons sour cream

1. Heat the olive oil in a soup pot over a moderate flame. Now, sauté the Spanish onion until tender and translucent.
2. Then, cook the garlic until just tender and aromatic. Stir in the butternut squash, celery, broth, salt, and black pepper.
3. Turn the heat to simmer and let it cook, covered, for 30 minutes. Fold in the baby spinach leaves and cover with the lid; let it sit in the residual heat until the baby
4. Spinach wilts completely. Serve dolloped with cold sour cream. Enjoy!

Per Serving

Calories: 150 | fat: 11.6g | protein: 2.5g | carbs: 6.8g | net carbs: 4.5g | fiber: 2.3g

Buffalo Mozzarella Cheesed Italian Peppers

Prep time: 7 minutes | Cook time: 13 minutes | Serves 5

- 4 tablespoons canola oil
- 1 yellow onion, sliced
- 1⅓ pounds (605 g) Italian peppers, seeded and sliced
- 1 teaspoon Italian
- seasoning mix
- Sea salt and cayenne pepper, to season
- 2 balls buffalo Mozzarella, drained and halved

1. Heat the canola oil in a saucepan over a medium-low flame.
2. Now, sauté the onion until just tender and translucent. Add in the peppers and spices. Cook for about 13 minutes, adding a splash of water to deglaze the pan.
3. Divide between serving plates; top with cheese and serve immediately. Enjoy!

Per Serving

Calories: 175 | fat: 11.0g | protein: 10.4g | carbs: 7.0g | net carbs: 5.1g | fiber: 1.9g

Crispy Bacon and Tender Brussels Sprouts

Prep time: 10 minutes | Cook time: 10 minutes | Serves 3

- 6 ounces (170 g) smoked bacon, diced
- 12 Brussels sprouts, trimmed and halved
- ¼ teaspoon ground bay leaf
- ¼ teaspoon dried oregano
- ¼ teaspoon dried sage
- ¼ teaspoon freshly cracked black pepper, or more to taste
- Sea salt, to taste
- ½ cup dry white wine
- 1 teaspoon Dijon mustard

1. Heat up a nonstick skillet over medium-high heat. Once hot, cook the bacon for 1 minute.
2. Add the Brussels sprouts and seasoning and continue sautéing, adding white wine and stirring until the bacon is crisp and the Brussels sprouts are tender. It will take about 9 minutes.
3. Then, stir in the mustard, remove from the heat, and serve immediately. Enjoy.

Per Serving

Calories: 298 | fat: 22.4g | protein: 9.6g | carbs: 6.4g | net carbs: 3.4g | fiber: 3.0g

Fennel Bulbs in Chicken Stock

Prep time: 10 minutes | Cook time: 20 minutes | Serves 6

- 2 tablespoons olive oil
- 1 celery stalk, chopped
- 1 pound (454 g) fennel bulbs, sliced
- 1 garlic clove, minced
- 1 bay laurel
- 1 thyme sprig
- 5 cups chicken stock
- Sea salt and ground black pepper, to season
- 2 eggs
- 1 tablespoon freshly squeezed lemon juice

1. Heat the olive oil in a heavy-bottomed pot over a medium-high flame. Sauté the celery and fennel until they have softened but not browned, about 8 minutes.

Vegetable Main

2. Add in the garlic, bay laurel, and thyme sprig; continue sautéing until aromatic an additional minute or so.

3. Add the chicken stock, salt, and black pepper to the pot. Bring to a boil. Reduce the heat to medium-low and let it simmer, partially covered, approximately 13 minutes. Discard the bay laurel and then, blend your soup with an immersion blender.

4. Whisk the eggs and lemon juice; gradually pour 2 cups of the hot soup into the egg mixture, whisking constantly. Return the soup to the pot and continue stirring for a few minutes or just until thickened. Serve warm.

Per Serving

Calories: 85 | fat: 6.2g | protein: 2.8g | carbs: 6.0g | net carbs: 3.5g | fiber: 2.5g

Dijon Mustard Chicken Mushrooms Skillet

Prep time: 10 minutes | Cook time: 20 minutes | Serves 6

- 2 cups sliced mushrooms
- ½ teaspoon onion powder
- ½ teaspoon garlic powder
- ¼ cup butter
- 1 teaspoon Dijon mustard
- 1 tablespoon tarragon, chopped
- 2 pounds (907 g) chicken thighs
- Salt and black pepper, to taste

1. Season the thighs with salt, pepper, garlic, and onion powder. Melt the butter in a skillet, and cook the chicken until browned; set aside.

2. Add mushrooms to the same fat and cook for about 5 minutes. Stir in Dijon mustard and ½ cup of water.

3. Return the chicken to the skillet. Season to taste with salt and pepper, reduce the heat and cover, and let simmer for 15 minutes. Stir in tarragon. Serve warm.

Per Serving

Calories: 405 | fat: 33g | protein: 25g | carbs: 1g | net carbs: 1g | fiber: 0g

Chicken Thighs in Coconut Cream

Prep time: 20 minutes | Cook time: 6 hours | Serves 6

- 3 tablespoons extra-virgin olive oil, divided
- 1 pound (454 g) boneless chicken thighs, diced into 1½-inch pieces
- ½ sweet onion, chopped
- 2 teaspoons minced garlic
- 2 cups chicken broth
- 2 celery stalks, diced
- 1 carrot, diced
- 1 teaspoon dried thyme
- 1 cup shredded kale
- 1 cup coconut cream
- Salt, for seasoning
- Freshly ground black pepper, for seasoning

1. Lightly grease the insert of the slow cooker with 1 tablespoon of the olive oil. In a large skillet over medium-high heat, heat the remaining 2 tablespoons of the olive oil.

2. Add the chicken and sauté until it is just cooked through, about 7 minutes. Add the onion and garlic and sauté for an additional 3 minutes. Transfer the chicken mixture to the insert, and stir in the broth, celery, carrot, and thyme.

3. Cover and cook on low for 6 hours. Stir in the kale and coconut cream. Season with salt and pepper, and serve warm.

Per Serving

Calories: 277 | fat: 22.0g | protein: 17.0g | carbs: 6.0g | net carbs: 4.0g | fiber: 2.0g

Creamy Cheesy Turkey Breast

Prep time: 10 minutes | Cook time: 25 minutes | Serves 5

- 3 teaspoons olive oil
- 1 cup bell peppers, sliced
- 1 yellow onion, thinly sliced
- 1½ pounds (680 g)
- turkey breast
- Sea salt and ground black pepper, to taste
- 1 cup chicken bone broth
- 1 cup double cream

- ½ cup Swiss cheese, shredded

1. Heat 2 teaspoons of the olive oil in a sauté pan over a moderate flame. Sauté the peppers and onion until they have softened; reserve.

2. In the same sauté pan, heat the remaining teaspoon of olive oil and sear the turkey breasts until no longer pink.

3. Layer the peppers and onions in a lightly greased baking pan. Add the turkey breast; sprinkle with salt and pepper.

4. Mix the chicken bone broth with the double cream; pour the mixture over the turkey breasts.

5. Bake in the preheated oven at 350°F (180°C) for 20 minutes; top with the Swiss cheese. Bake an additional 5 minutes or until golden brown on top.

Per Serving

Calories: 465 | fat: 28.5g | protein: 45.4g | carbs: 4.5g | net carbs: 4.2g | fiber: 0.3g

Oriental Sweets Pepper Turkey Soup

Prep time: 10 minutes | Cook time: 15 minutes | Serves 5

- 2 tablespoons canola oil
- 2 Oriental sweets peppers, deseeded and chopped
- 1 Bird's eye chili, deseeded and chopped
- 2 green onions, chopped
- 5 cups vegetable broth
- 1 pound (454 g) turkey thighs, deboned and cut into halves
- ½ teaspoon five-spice powder
- 1 teaspoon oyster sauce
- Kosher salt, to taste

1. Heat the olive oil in a stockpot over a moderate flame. Then, sauté the peppers and onions until they have softened or about 4 minutes.

2. Add in the other ingredients and bring to a boil. Turn the heat to simmer, cover, and continue to cook an additional 12 minutes. Ladle into individual bowls and serve warm. Enjoy!

Per Serving

Calories: 180 | fat: 7.5g | protein: 21.4g | carbs: 6.7g | net carbs: 5.5g | fiber: 1.2g

Boneless Chicken in Dry Sherry Wine

Prep time: 10 minutes | Cook time: 10 minutes | Serves 6

- 2 tablespoons olive oil
- 4 tablespoons dry sherry
- 1 tablespoon stone-ground mustard
- 1½ pounds (680 g) chicken, skinless, boneless and cubed
- 2 red onions, cut into wedges
- 1 green bell pepper, cut into 1-inch pieces
- 1 red bell pepper, cut into 1-inch pieces
- 1 yellow bell pepper, cut into 1-inch pieces
- ½ teaspoon sea salt
- ¼ teaspoon ground black pepper, or more to taste

1. In a mixing bowl, combine the olive oil, dry sherry, mustard and chicken until well coated. Alternate skewering the chicken and vegetables until you run out of ingredients.

2. Season with salt and black pepper.

3. Preheat your grill to medium-high heat. Place the kabobs on the grill, flipping every 2 minutes and cook to desired doneness. Serve warm.

Per Serving

Calories: 201 | fat: 8.2g | protein: 24.3g | carbs:7.0 g | net carbs: 5.7g | fiber: 1.3g

Delicious Chicken Capocollo Bake

Prep time: 5 minutes | Cook time: 35 minutes | Serves 5

- 2 pounds (907 g) chicken drumsticks, skinless and boneless
- 1 garlic clove, peeled and halved
- ½ teaspoon smoked
- paprika
- Coarse sea salt and ground black pepper, to taste
- 10 thin slices of capocollo

1. Using a sharp kitchen knife, butterfly cut the chicken drumsticks in half. Lay each chicken drumstick flat on a cutting board and rub garlic halves over the surface of chicken drumsticks.

2. Season with paprika, salt, and black pepper. Lay a

slice of capocollo on each piece, pressing lightly.

3. Roll them up and secure with toothpicks. Bake in the preheated oven at 420°F (216°C) for about 15 minutes until the edges of the chicken begin to brown. Turnover and bake for a further 15 to 20 minutes.

Per Serving

Calories: 486 | fat: 33.7g | protein: 39.1g | carbs: 3.6g | net carbs: 2.6g | fiber: 1.0g

Cinnamon Spiced Duck in Veggie Broth

Prep time: 15 minutes | Cook time: 25 minutes | Serves 3

- 2 teaspoons canola oil
- 1 red bell pepper, seeded and chopped
- 1 shallot, chopped
- ½ cup celery rib, chopped
- ½ cup chayote, peeled and cubed
- 1 pound (454 g) duck breasts, boneless, skinless, and chopped
- into small chunks
- 1½ cups vegetable broth
- ½ stick Mexican cinnamon
- 1 thyme sprig
- 1 rosemary sprig
- Sea salt and freshly ground black pepper, to taste

1. Heat the canola oil in a soup pot (or clay pot) over a medium-high flame. Now, sauté the bell pepper, shallot and celery until they have softened about 5 minutes.

2. Add the remaining ingredients and stir to combine. Once it starts boiling, turn the heat to simmer and partially cover the pot.

3. Let it simmer for 17 to 20 minutes or until thoroughly cooked. Enjoy.

Per Serving

Calories: 230 | fat: 9.6g | protein: 30.5g | carbs: 3.3g | net carbs: 2.3g | fiber: 1.0g

Chapter 5: Smoothies

Coconut Milk Spinach Berry Smoothie

Prep time: 5 minutes | Cook time: 0 minutes | Serves 2

- 1 cup coconut milk
- 1 cup spinach
- ½ English cucumber, chopped
- ½ cup blueberries
- 1 scoop plain protein
- powder
- 2 tablespoons coconut oil
- 4 ice cubes
- Mint sprigs, for garnish

1. Put the coconut milk, spinach, cucumber, blueberries, protein powder, coconut oil, and ice in a blender and blend until smooth.

2. Pour into 2 glasses, garnish each with the mint, and serve immediately.

Per Serving

Calories: 353 | fat: 32g | protein: 15g | carbs: 9g | net carbs: 6g | fiber: 3g

Vanilla Flavoured Coconut Milk Smoothie

Prep time: 5 minutes | Cook time: 0 minutes | Serves 2

- 2 cups coconut milk
- 1 scoop vanilla protein powder
- 5 drops liquid stevia
- 1 teaspoon ground cinnamon
- ½ teaspoon alcohol-free vanilla extract

1. Put the coconut milk, protein powder, stevia, cinnamon, and vanilla in a blender and blend until smooth.

2. Pour into 2 glasses and serve immediately.

Per Serving

Calories: 492 | fat: 47g | protein: 18g | carbs: 8g | net carbs: 6g | fiber: 2g

Vanilla Bone Broth Protein Smoothie

Prep time: 5 minutes | Cook time: 0 minutes | Serves 1

- 1 cup full-fat coconut milk
- ½ teaspoon vanilla extract
- 1 scoop vanilla bone broth protein
- ½ cup water
- 1 cup ice
- Pinch of sea salt
- 2 to 3 drops liquid stevia (optional)

1. Place all the ingredients in a high-speed blender and blend until smooth.

Per Serving

Calories: 549 | fat: 49g | protein: 25g | carbs: 9g | net carbs: 9g | fiber: 0g

Chocolaty Spinach Smoothie

Prep time: 5 minutes | Cook time: 0 minutes | Serves 1

- 1 cup frozen spinach
- 1 cup unsweetened almond milk
- 2 tablespoons hemp hearts
- 1 tablespoon MCT oil
- 1 scoop chocolate-flavored protein powder

1. Put all the ingredients in a blender and blend until smooth, 30 to 45 seconds.
2. Pour into a glass and serve immediately.

Per Serving

Calories: 416 | fat: 27g | protein: 35g | carbs: 7g | net carbs: 4g | fiber: 3g

Delicious Chocolaty Almond Smoothie

Prep time: 5 minutes | Cook time: 0 minutes | Serves 2

- ⅓ ripe avocado, peeled and pitted
- 3 teaspoons cacao powder, unsweetened
- ¼ teaspoon grated nutmeg
- 2 teaspoons granulated erythritol

- 1 cup almond milk
- ½ cup water

1. Purée all ingredients in a blender until smooth and uniform.
2. Spoon into two glasses and enjoy!

Per Serving

Calories: 140 | fat: 9g | protein: 4g | carbs: 7g | net carbs: 4g | fiber: 3g

Seeds and Coconut Milk Smoothie

Prep time: 5 minutes | Cook time: 0 minutes | Serves 2

- ½ ripe avocado, peeled and pitted
- ½ cup canned coconut milk
- ½ cup water
- 2 teaspoons sunflower seeds
- 2 tablespoons sesame seeds
- 2 teaspoons granulated erythritol
- 1 teaspoon ground cinnamon

1. Purée all the ingredients in your blender or food processor.
2. Divide the mixture between two serving bowls and serve well-chilled.

Per Serving

Calories: 286 | fat: 28g | protein: 5g | carbs: 8g | net carbs: 5g | fiber: 3g

Chapter 6: Pork

Citrusy Pork Chops

Prep time: 10 minutes | Cook time: 15 minutes | Serves 4

- 1 pound (454 g) boneless center-cut pork chops, pounded to ¼ inch thick
- Sea salt, for seasoning
- Freshly ground black pepper, for seasoning
- ¼ cup good-quality olive oil, divided
- ¼ cup finely chopped fresh cilantro
- 1 tablespoon minced garlic
- Juice of 1 lime

1. Marinate the pork. Pat the pork chops dry and season them lightly with salt and pepper.

2. Place them in a large bowl, add 2 tablespoons of the olive oil, and the cilantro, garlic, and lime juice. Toss to coat the chops. Cover the bowl and marinate the chops at room temperature for 30 minutes.

3. Cook the pork. In a large skillet over medium-high heat, warm the remaining 2 tablespoons of olive oil.

4. Add the pork chops in a single layer and fry them, turning them once, until they're just cooked through and still juicy, 6 to 7 minutes per side.

5. Serve. Divide the chops between four plates and serve them immediately.

Per Serving

Calories: 249 | fat: 16g | protein: 25g | carbs: 2g | net carbs: 2g | fiber: 0g

Oregano Herbed Pork Chops with Salsa

Prep time: 15 minutes | Cook time: 15 minutes | Serves 4

- ¼ cup good-quality olive oil, divided
- 1 tablespoon red wine vinegar
- 3 teaspoons chopped fresh oregano, divided
- 1 teaspoon minced garlic
- 4 (4-ounce / 113-g) boneless center-cut loin pork chops
- ½ cup halved cherry tomatoes
- ½ yellow bell pepper, diced
- ½ English cucumber, chopped
- ¼ red onion, chopped
- 1 tablespoon balsamic vinegar
- Sea salt, for seasoning
- Freshly ground black pepper, for seasoning

1. Marinate the pork. In a medium bowl, stir together 3 tablespoons of the olive oil, the vinegar, 2 teaspoons of the oregano, and the garlic. Add the pork chops to the bowl, turning them to get them coated with the marinade. Cover the bowl and place it in the refrigerator for 30 minutes.

2. Make the salsa. While the pork is marinating, in a medium bowl, stir together the remaining 1

tablespoon of olive oil, the tomatoes, yellow bell pepper, cucumber, red onion, vinegar, and the remaining 1 teaspoon of oregano. Season the salsa with salt and pepper. Set the bowl aside.

3. Grill the pork chops. Heat a grill to medium-high heat. Remove the pork chops from the marinade and grill them until just cooked through, 6 to 8 minutes per side.

4. Serve. Rest the pork for 5 minutes. Divide the pork between four plates and serve them with a generous scoop of the salsa.

Per Serving

Calories: 277 | fat: 17g | protein: 25g | carbs: 4g | net carbs: 3g | fiber: 1g

Garlicky Pork Beef Bake

Prep time: 5 minutes | Cook time: 13 minutes | Serves 5

- 1 pound (454 g) ground pork
- ½ pound (227 g) ground beef
- Onion, chopped
- Garlic cloves, minced
- 1 teaspoon Hungarian spice blend

1. In a mixing bowl, thoroughly combine all ingredients until they are well incorporated. Form the mixture into meatballs with oiled hands. Place your meatballs on a tinfoil-lined baking sheet.

2. Bake in the preheated oven at 395°F (202°C) for 12 to 14 minutes or until they are golden brown.

3. Arrange on a nice serving platter and serve.

Per Serving

Calories: 377 | fat: 24g | protein: 36g | carbs: 2g | net carbs: 2g | fiber: 0g

Hot and Spicy Pork Pot

Prep time: 10 minutes | Cook time: 1 hour | Serves 5

- 2 tablespoons olive oil
- 2 pounds pork stew meat
- 1 yellow onion, chopped
- 1 garlic cloves, minced
- ¼ cup dry sherry wine
- 4 cups chicken bone broth
- 1 cup tomatoes,

- pureed
- 1 bay laurel
- Sea salt and ground
- black pepper, to taste
- 1 tablespoon fresh cilantro, chopped

1. Heat the olive oil in a soup pot over a moderate flame. Sear the pork for about 5 minutes, stirring continuously to ensure even cooking; reserve.

2. Cook the yellow onion in the pan drippings until just tender and translucent. Stir in the garlic and continue to sauté for a further 30 seconds.

3. Pour in a splash of dry sherry to deglaze the pan.

4. Pour in the chicken bone broth and bring to a boil. Stir in the tomatoes and bay laurel. Season with salt and pepper to taste. Turn the heat to medium-low and continue to cook 10 minutes longer.

5. Add the reserved pork back to the pot, partially cover, and continue to simmer for 45 minutes longer.

6. Garnish with cilantro and serve hot.

Per Serving

Calories: 332 | fat: 15g | protein: 41g | carbs: 4g | net carbs: 3g | fiber: 1g

Healthy Low Carb Pork Burger

Prep time: 10 minutes | Cook time: 5 minutes | Serves 6

- 2 pound (907 g) ground pork
- Pink salt and chili pepper, to taste
- 1 tablespoon olive oil
- 1 tablespoon butter
- 1 white onion, sliced into rings
- 1 tablespoon balsamic vinegar
- 3 drops liquid stevia
- 6 low carb burger buns, halved
- 2 firm tomatoes, sliced into rings

1. Combine the pork, salt and chili pepper in a bowl, and mold out 6 patties.

2. Heat the olive oil in a skillet over medium heat, and fry the patties for 4 to 5 minutes on each side until golden brown on the outside. Remove onto a plate, and sit for 3 minutes.

3. Melt butter in a skillet over medium heat, sauté onions for 2 minutes, and stir in the balsamic

vinegar and liquid stevia. Cook for 30 seconds stirring once, or twice until caramelized. In each bun, place a patty, top with some onion rings and 2 tomato rings.

4. Serve the burgers with cheddar cheese dip.

Per Serving

Calories: 315 | fat: 23g | protein: 16g | carbs: 7g | net carbs: 6g | fiber: 1g

Baked Beans and Pork

Prep time: 10 minutes | Cook time: 40 minutes | Serves 4

- 1 pound (454 g) ground pork
- 1 onion, chopped
- 1 garlic clove, minced
- ½ green beans, chopped
- Salt and black pepper,
- to taste
- 1 zucchini, sliced
- ¼ cup heavy cream
- 5 eggs
- ½ cup Monterey Jack cheese, grated

1. In a bowl, mix onion, green beans, ground pork, garlic, black pepper and salt. Layer the meat mixture on the bottom of a small greased baking dish. Spread zucchini slices on top.

2. In a separate bowl, combine cheese, eggs and heavy cream. Top with this creamy mixture and bake for 40 minutes at 360°F (182°C), until the edges and top become brown.

3. Serve immediately.

Per Serving

Calories: 335 | fat: 21g | protein: 28g | carbs: 4g | net carbs: 4g | fiber: 0g

Pork Veggie Lettuce Wraps

Prep time: 10 minutes | Cook time: 14 minutes | Serves 6

- 2 pound (907 g) ground pork
- 1 tablespoon ginger-garlic paste
- Pink salt and chili pepper, to taste
- 1 teaspoon butter
- 1 fresh head iceberg lettuce
- 2 sprigs green onion, chopped
- 1 red bell pepper,

chopped　　　　　　　　chopped

- ½ cucumber, finely

1. Put the pork with ginger-garlic, salt, and chili pepper seasoning in a saucepan. Cook for 10 minutes over medium heat while breaking any lumps until the beef is no longer pink.

2. Drain liquid and add the butter, melt, and brown the meat for 4 minutes with continuous stirring. Pat the lettuce dry with paper towel and in each leaf spoon two to three tablespoons of pork, top with green onions, bell pepper, and cucumber.

3. Serve with soy drizzling sauce.

Per Serving

Calories: 311 | fat: 24g | protein: 19g | carbs: 3g | net carbs: 1g | fiber: 2g

Grilled BBQ Pork

Prep time: 10 minutes | Cook time: 50 minutes | Serves 4

- 1 tablespoon erythritol
- Salt and black pepper, to taste
- 1 tablespoon olive oil
- 1 teaspoon chipotle powder
- 1 teaspoon garlic powder
- 1 pound (454 g) pork spare ribs
- 1 tablespoon sugar-free BBQ sauce

1. Mix the erythritol, salt, pepper, oil, chipotle, and garlic powder. Brush on the meaty sides of the ribs, and wrap in foil. Sit for 30 minutes to marinate.

2. Preheat oven to 400°F (205°C), place wrapped ribs on a baking sheet, and cook for 40 minutes to be cooked through.

3. Remove ribs and aluminum foil, brush with BBQ sauce, and brown under the broiler for 10 minutes on both sides. Slice and serve with extra BBQ sauce and lettuce tomato salad.

Per Serving

Calories: 294 | fat: 18g | protein: 28g | carbs: 3g | net carbs: 3g | fiber: 0g

Chili spiced Pork Chops

Prep time: 10 minutes | Cook time: 9 minutes |

Serves 4

- 4 pork chops
- 1 tablespoon olive oil
- 1 garlic clove, minced
- ¼ tablespoon chili powder
- ¼ teaspoon cumin
- Salt and black pepper, to taste
- ½ teaspoon hot pepper sauce
- ¼ cup capers
- 6 black olives, sliced

1. Preheat grill over medium heat. In a mixing bowl, combine olive oil, cumin, salt, hot pepper sauce, pepper, garlic and chili powder.

2. Place in the pork chops, toss to coat, and refrigerate for 4 hours.

3. Arrange the pork on a preheated grill, cook for 7 minutes, turn, add in the capers, and cook for another 2 minutes. Place onto serving plates and sprinkle with olives to serve.

Per Serving

Calories: 300 | fat: 14g | protein: 40g | carbs: 2g | net carbs: 1g | fiber: 1g

One Pan Herbed Pork with Tomatoes

Prep time: 10 minutes | Cook time: 37 minutes | Serves 4

- 4 pork chops
- ½ tablespoon fresh basil, chopped
- 1 garlic clove, minced
- 1 tablespoon olive oil
- 7 ounces (198 g) canned dice tomatoes
- ½ tablespoon tomato purée
- Salt and black pepper, to taste
- ½ red chili, finely chopped

1. Season the pork with salt and black pepper. Set a pan over medium heat and warm oil, place in the pork chops, cook for 3 minutes, turn and cook for another 3 minutes; remove to a bowl. Add in the garlic and cook for 30 seconds.

2. Stir in the tomato purée, tomatoes, and chili; bring to a boil, and reduce heat to medium-low. Place in the pork chops, cover the pan and simmer everything for 30 minutes.

3. Remove the pork chops to plates and sprinkle with fresh oregano to serve.

Calories: 372 | fat: 21g | protein: 40g | carbs: 3g | net carbs: 2g | fiber: 1g

Citrusy Pork Chops with Parsley

Prep time: 10 minutes | Cook time: 12 minutes | Serves 4

- 1 tablespoon olive oil
- 1 tablespoon lemon juice
- 1 garlic clove, pureed
- 4 pork loin chops
- ⅓ head cabbage, shredded
- 1 tomato, chopped
- 1 tablespoon white wine
- Salt and black pepper, to taste
- ¼ teaspoon cumin
- ¼ teaspoon ground nutmeg
- 1 tablespoon parsley

1. In a bowl, mix the lemon juice, garlic, salt, pepper and olive oil. Brush the pork with the mixture.
2. Preheat grill to high heat. Grill the pork for 2to 3 minutes on each side until cooked through.
3. Remove to serving plates. Warm the remaining olive oil in a pan and cook in cabbage for 5 minutes.
4. Drizzle with white wine, sprinkle with cumin, nutmeg, salt and pepper. Add in the tomatoes; cook for another 5 minutes, stirring occasionally. Ladle the sautéed cabbage to the side of the chops and serve sprinkled with parsley.

Per Serving

Calories: 382 | fat: 21g | protein: 41g | carbs: 6g | net carbs: 4g | fiber: 2g

Pork Steaks in Chimichurri Sauce

Prep time: 10 minutes | Cook time: 5 minutes | Serves 4

- 1 garlic clove, minced
- ½ teaspoon white wine vinegar
- 1 tablespoon parsley
- leaves, chopped
- 1 tablespoon cilantro leaves, chopped
- 1 tablespoon extra-

- virgin olive oil
- 16 ounces (454 g) pork loin steaks
- Salt and black pepper, to taste
- 1 tablespoon sesame oil

1. To make the sauce: in a bowl, mix the parsley, cilantro and garlic. Add the vinegar, extra-virgin olive oil, and salt, and combine well.
2. Preheat a grill pan over medium heat. Rub the pork with sesame oil, and season with salt and pepper. Grill the meat for 4 to 5 minutes on each side until no longer pink in the center.
3. Put the pork on a serving plate and spoon chimichurri sauce over, to serve.

Per Serving

Calories: 326 | fat: 21g | protein: 32g | carbs: 2g | net carbs: 2g | fiber: 0g

Pork Chops in Worcestershire Sauce

Prep time: 10 minutes | Cook time: 10 minutes | Serves 4

- 1 tablespoon olive oil
- 1 pound (454 g) pork chops
- Salt and black pepper, to taste
- 1 cup blackberries
- 1 tablespoon chicken broth
- ½ tablespoon rosemary leaves, chopped
- 1 tablespoon balsamic vinegar
- 1 teaspoon Worcestershire sauce

1. Place the blackberries in a bowl and mash them with a fork until jam-like. Pour into a sauce pan; add the chicken broth and rosemary.
2. Bring to boil on low heat for 4 minutes. Stir in balsamic vinegar and Worcestershire sauce. Simmer for 1 minute.
3. Heat oil in a skillet over medium heat, season the pork with salt and black pepper, and cook for 5 minutes on each side. Put on serving plates and spoon sauce over the pork chops.

Per Serving

Calories: 302 | fat: 18g | protein: 28g | carbs: 4g | net carbs: 2g | fiber: 2g

Rosemary Herbed Brown Pork

Prep time: 10 minutes | Cook time: 20 minutes | Serves 4

- 2 onions, chopped
- 4 ounces (113 g) bacon, chopped
- ½ cup vegetable stock
- Salt and black pepper, to taste
- 1 tablespoon fresh rosemary, chopped
- 1 pound (454 g) pork medallions

1. Fry the bacon in a pan over medium heat, until crispy, and remove to a plate.
2. Add in onions, black pepper, and salt, and cook for 5 minutes; set to the same plate with bacon.
3. Add pork to the pan, brown for 3 minutes, turn, and cook for 7 minutes. Stir in stock and cook for 2 minutes. Return bacon and onions to the pan and cook for 1 minute. Garnish with rosemary.

Per Serving

Calories: 258 | fat: 15g | protein: 23g | carbs: 8g | net carbs: 6g | fiber: 2g

Pork Stew with Cauliflower Florets

Prep time: 15 minutes | Cook time: 30 minutes | Serves 4

- 1 tablespoon olive oil
- 1 red bell pepper, chopped
- 1 pound (454 g) stewed pork, cubed
- Salt and black pepper, to taste
- 2 cups cauliflower florets
- 2 cups broccoli florets
- 1 onion, chopped
- 14 ounces (397 g) canned dice tomatoes
- ¼ teaspoon garlic powder
- 1 tablespoon tomato puree
- 1½ cups water
- 1 tablespoon parsley, chopped

1. In a pan, heat olive oil and cook the pork over medium heat for 5 minutes, until browned.
2. Place in the bell pepper, and onion, and cook for 4 minutes. Stir in the water, tomatoes, broccoli, cauliflower, tomato purée, and garlic powder;

bring to a simmer and cook for 20minutes while covered. Adjust the seasoning and serve sprinkled with parsley.

Per Serving

Calories: 299 | fat: 13g | protein: 35g | carbs: 10g | net carbs: 6g | fiber: 4g

Chapter 7: Beef and Lamb

Cheesy Beef Steak with Baby Spinach

Prep time: 5 minutes | Cook time: 15 minutes | Serves 6

- 1½ pounds (680 g) beef flank steak
- Salt and black pepper, to season
- ⅔ cup feta cheese, crumbled
- ½ loose cup baby spinach
- 1 jalapeño pepper, chopped
- ¼ cup basil leaves, chopped

1. Preheat oven to 400°F (205°C). Grease a baking sheet with cooking spray.
2. Wrap the steak in plastic wrap, place on a flat surface, and gently run a rolling pin over to flatten. Take off the wraps.
3. Sprinkle with half of the feta cheese, top with spinach, jalapeño, basil leaves, and the remaining cheese. Carefully roll the steak over on the stuffing and secure with toothpicks.
4. Place in the greased baking sheet, and cook for 15 minutes, flipping once until nicely browned on the outside and the cheese melted within. Cool for 3 minutes, slice into pinwheels, and serve.

Per Serving

Calories: 199 | fat: 9g | protein: 27g | carbs: 1g | net carbs: 1g | fiber: 0g

Garlic Beef with Shirataki rice

Prep time: 5 minutes | Cook time: 21 minutes | Serves 6

- 1 tablespoon olive oil
- 1½ pounds (680 g) ground beef
- 1 tablespoon ginger-garlic paste
- 1 teaspoon garam masala
- 1 (7-ounce / 198-g) can whole tomatoes
- 1 small head cauliflower, cut into florets
- Pink salt and chili pepper, to taste
- ¼ cup water

1. Heat oil in a saucepan over medium heat; add in beef, ginger-garlic paste and season with garam masala. Cook for 5 minutes while breaking any lumps.
2. Stir in tomatoes and cauliflower, season with salt and chili pepper, and cook for 6 minutes.
3. Add the water and bring to a boil over medium heat for 10 minutes, or until the liquid has reduced by half.
4. Adjust taste with salt. Serve with shirataki rice.

Per Serving

Calories: 255 | fat: 17g | protein: 23g | carbs: 4g | net carbs: 2g | fiber: 2g

Beef Mushroom Meatloaf

Prep time: 15 minutes | Cook time: 1 hour 10 minutes | Serves 12

- 3 pounds (1.4 kg) ground beef
- ½ cup onion, chopped
- ½ cup almond flour
- 2 garlic cloves, minced
- 1 cup mushrooms, sliced
- 3 eggs
- Salt and black pepper, to taste
- 2 tablespoons parsley, chopped
- ¼ cup bell peppers, chopped
- ⅓ cup Parmesan cheese, grated
- 1 teaspoon balsamic vinegar

Glaze:

- 2 cups balsamic vinegar
- 1 tablespoon sweetener
- 2 tablespoons tomato purée

1. Combine all of the meatloaf ingredients in a large bowl. Press the mixture into greased loaf pan.
2. Bake at 375°F (190°C) for about 30 minutes. Make the glaze by combining all of the ingredients in a saucepan over medium heat.
3. Simmer for 20 minutes, until the glaze is thickened. Pour ¼ cup of the glaze over the meatloaf. Save the extra for future use. Put the meatloaf back in the oven, and cook for 20 more minutes.

Per Serving

Calories: 375 | fat: 25g | protein: 23g | carbs: 13g | net carbs: 12g | fiber: 1g

Thai Green Beef Curry

Prep time: 10 minutes | Cook time: 24 minutes | Serves 4

- ½ cup coconut milk
- 2 tablespoons coconut oil
- ¼ teaspoon garlic powder
- ¼ teaspoon onion powder
- ½ tablespoon coconut amino
- 1 pound (454 g) beef steak, cut into strips
- Salt and black pepper, to taste
- 1 head broccoli, cut into florets
- ½ tablespoon Thai green curry paste
- 1 teaspoon ginger paste
- 1 tablespoon cilantro, chopped
- ½ tablespoon sesame seeds

1. Warm coconut oil in a pan over medium heat, add in beef, season with garlic powder, pepper, salt, ginger paste and onion powder and cook for 4 minutes. Mix in the broccoli and stir-fry for 5 minutes.
2. Pour in the coconut milk, coconut amino, and Thai curry paste and cook for 15 minutes.
3. Serve sprinkled with cilantro and sesame seeds.

Per Serving

Calories: 350 | fat: 22g | protein: 30g | carbs: 13g | net carbs: 8g | fiber: 5g

Sautéed Beef Onion Tomato Skillet

Prep time: 5 minutes | Cook time: 22 minutes | Serves 6

- 1½ pounds (680 g) beef tripe
- 4 cups coconut milk
- Pink salt, to taste
- 2 teaspoons Creole
- seasoning
- 3 tablespoons olive oil
- 2 onions, sliced
- 3 tomatoes, diced

1. Put tripe in a bowl, and cover with coconut milk. Refrigerate for 3 hours to extract bitterness and gamey taste.
2. Remove from coconut milk, pat dry with paper towels, and season with salt and creole seasoning.
3. Heat 2 tablespoons of oil in a skillet over medium heat and brown the tripe on both sides for 6 minutes in total. Remove, and set aside.
4. Add the remaining oil and sauté onions for 3 minutes. Include the tomatoes and cook for 10 minutes. Put the tripe in the sauce, and cook for 3 minutes.

Per Serving

Calories: 284 | fat: 16g | protein: 20g | carbs: 14g | net carbs: 12g | fiber: 2g

Sirloin Steak Veggies Salad

Prep time: 10 minutes | Cook time: 13 minutes | Serves 4

- 1 pound (454 g) sirloin steak, boneless, cubed
- ¼ cup ranch dressing
- 1 red onion, sliced
- ½ tablespoon white wine vinegar
- 1 tablespoon extra-
- virgin olive oil
- 2 ripe tomatoes, sliced
- 2 tablespoons fresh parsley, chopped
- 1 cucumber, sliced
- Salt, to taste

1. Thread the beef cubes on the skewers, about 4-5 cubes per skewer. Brush half of the ranch dressing on the skewers (all around).
2. Preheat grill to 400°F (205°C) and place the skewers on the grill grate to cook for 6 minutes. Turn the skewers once and cook further for 6

minutes.

3. Brush the remaining ranch dressing on the meat and cook them for 1 more minute on each side.
4. In a salad bowl mix together red onion, tomatoes, and cucumber, sprinkle with salt, vinegar, and extra-virgin olive oil; toss to combine. Top the salad with skewers and scatter the parsley all over.

Per Serving

Calories: 357 | fat: 23g | protein: 25g | carbs: 12g | net carbs: 10g | fiber: 2g

Crispy Beef Burgers with Parsley

Prep time: 5 minutes | Cook time: 18 minutes | Serves 4

- 2 tablespoons olive oil
- 1 pound (454 g) ground beef
- 2 green onions, chopped
- 1 garlic clove, minced
- 1 tablespoon thyme
- 2 tablespoons almond
- flour
- 2 tablespoons beef broth
- ½ tablespoon chopped parsley
- ½ tablespoon Worcestershire sauce

1. Grease a baking dish with the olive oil. Combine all ingredients except for the parsley in a bowl.
2. Mix well with your hands and make 2 patties out of the mixture. Arrange on a lined baking sheet.
3. Bake at 370°F (188°C), for about 18 minutes, until nice and crispy. Serve sprinkled with parsley.

Per Serving

Calories: 371 | fat: 30g | protein: 20g | carbs: 5g | net carbs: 4g | fiber: 1g

Thyme Herbed Beef Brisket in Wine

Prep time: 10 minutes | Cook time: 2 hours | Serves 4

- 1 tablespoon olive oil
- 1 pound (454 g) brisket
- 1 red onion, quartered
- 2 stalks celery, cut into chunks
- 1 garlic clove, minced

- Salt and black pepper, to taste
- 1 bay leaf
- 1 tablespoon fresh thyme, chopped
- 1 cup red wine

1. Season the brisket with salt and pepper. Brown the meat on both sides in warm olive oil over medium heat for 6-8 minutes. Transfer to a deep casserole dish.

2. In the dish, arrange the onion, garlic, celery, and bay leaf around the brisket and pour the wine all over it.

3. Cover the pot and cook the ingredients in the oven for 2 hours at 370°F (188°C). When ready, remove the casserole.

4. Transfer the beef to a chopping board and cut it into thick slices. Serve the beef and vegetables with a drizzle of the sauce.

Per Serving

Calories: 203 | fat: 9g | protein: 25g | carbs: 3g | net carbs: 2g | fiber: 1g

Heavy Creamed Beef Steak

Prep time: 15 minutes | Cook time: 17 minutes | Serves 4

- 2 garlic cloves, minced
- 2 tablespoons butter
- 2 tablespoons olive oil
- 1 tablespoon fresh rosemary, chopped
- 1 pound (454 g) beef rump steak, sliced
- Salt and black pepper, to taste
- 1 shallot, chopped
- ½ cup heavy cream
- ½ cup beef stock
- 1 tablespoon mustard
- 2 teaspoons coconut amino
- 2 teaspoons lemon juice
- 1 teaspoon xylitol
- A sprig of rosemary
- A sprig of thyme

1. Set a pan to medium heat, warm in a tablespoon of olive oil and stir in the shallot; cook for 3 minutes.

2. Stir in the stock, coconut amino, xylitol, thyme sprig, cream, mustard and rosemary sprig, and cook for 8 minutes. Stir in butter, lemon juice, pepper and salt. Get rid of the rosemary and thyme. Set aside.

3. In a bowl, combine the remaining oil with black pepper, garlic, rosemary, and salt. Toss in the beef to coat, and set aside for some minutes.

4. Heat a pan over medium-high heat, place in the beef steak, and cook for 6 minutes, flipping halfway through; set aside and keep warm. Plate the beef slices, sprinkle over the sauce, and enjoy.

Per Serving

Calories: 339 | fat: 25g | protein: 26g | carbs: 3g | net carbs: 2g | fiber: 1g

Ricotta Cheesed Steak Kale Roll

Prep time: 10 minutes | Cook time: 30 minutes | Serves 4

- 1 pound (454 g) flank steak
- Salt and black pepper, to taste
- ½ cup ricotta cheese, crumbled
- ½ cup baby kale, chopped
- 1 serrano pepper, chopped
- 1 tablespoon basil leaves, chopped

1. Wrap the steak in plastic wraps, place on a flat surface, and gently run a rolling pin over to flatten. Take off the wraps.

2. Sprinkle with half of the ricotta cheese, top with kale, Serrano pepper, and the remaining cheese. Roll the steak over on the stuffing and secure with toothpicks.

3. Place in the greased baking sheet and cook for 30 minutes at 390°F (199°C), flipping once until nicely browned on the outside and the cheese melted within. Cool for 3 minutes, slice and serve with basil.

Per Serving

Calories: 211 | fat: 10g | protein: 28g | carbs: 1g | net carbs: 1g | fiber: 0g

Beef Chuck Roast Mushroom Bake

Prep time: 15 minutes | Cook time: 1 hour 35 minutes | Serves 4

- 2 tablespoons olive oil
- 1 pound (454 g) beef chuck roast, cubed
- 1 cup canned diced tomatoes
- Salt and black pepper, to taste

- ½ pound (227 g) mushrooms, sliced
- 1 celery stalk, chopped
- 1 bell pepper, sliced
- 1 onion, chopped
- 1 bay leaf
- ½ cup beef stock
- 1 tablespoon fresh rosemary, chopped
- ½ teaspoon dry mustard
- 1 tablespoon almond flour

1. Preheat oven to 350°F (180°C). Set a pot over medium heat, warm olive oil and brown the beef on each side for 4-5 minutes.
1. Stir in tomatoes, onion, mustard, mushrooms, bell pepper, celery, and stock. Season with salt and pepper.
1. In a bowl, combine ½ cup of water with flour and stir in the pot. Transfer to a baking dish and bake for 90 minutes, stirring at intervals of 30 minutes. Scatter the rosemary over and serve warm.

Per Serving

Calories: 329 | fat: 17g | protein: 34g | carbs: 8g | net carbs: 4g | fiber: 4g

Chuck Steak with Green Beans

Prep time: 15 minutes | Cook time: 1 hour 48 minutes | Serves 4

- 2 tablespoons olive oil
- 1 pound (454 g) chuck steak, cubed
- Salt and black pepper, to taste
- 2 tablespoons almond flour
- 4 green onions, diced
- ½ cup dry white wine
- 1 yellow bell pepper, diced
- 1 cup green beans, chopped
- 2 teaspoons Worcestershire sauce
- 4 ounces (113 g) tomato purée
- 3 teaspoons smoked paprika
- 1 cup beef broth
- Parsley leaves, for garnish

1. Dredge the meat in the almond flour and set aside. Place a large skillet over medium heat, add 1 tablespoon of oil to heat and then sauté the green onion, green beans, and bell pepper for 3 minutes. Stir in the paprika and the remaining olive oil.
2. Add the beef and cook for 10 minutes while turning them halfway. Stir in white wine, let it reduce by half, about 3 minutes, and add Worcestershire sauce, tomato purée, and beef broth.
3. Let the mixture boil for 2 minutes, then reduce the heat to lowest and let simmer for 1½ hours; stirring now and then.
4. Adjust the taste and dish the ragout. Serve garnished with parsley leaves.

Per Serving

Calories: 302 | fat: 17g | protein: 27g | carbs: 12g | net carbs: 9g | fiber: 3g

Spicy Beef Cauliflower Curry

Prep time: 10 minutes | Cook time: 21 minutes | Serves 4

- 1 tablespoon olive oil
- ½ pound (227 g) ground beef
- 1 garlic clove, minced
- 1 teaspoon turmeric
- 1 tablespoon cilantro, chopped
- 1 tablespoon ginger paste
- ½ teaspoon garam masala
- 5 ounces (142 g) canned whole tomatoes
- 1 head cauliflower, cut into florets
- Salt and chili pepper, to taste
- ¼ cup water

1. Heat oil in a saucepan over medium heat; add the beef, garlic, ginger paste, and garam masala. Cook for 5 minutes while breaking any lumps.
2. Stir in the tomatoes and cauliflower, season with salt, turmeric, and chili pepper, and cook covered for 6 minutes.
3. Add the water and bring to a boil over medium heat for 10 minutes or until the water has reduced by half. Spoon the curry into serving bowls and serve sprinkled with cilantro.

Per Serving

Calories: 201 | fat: 15g | protein: 11g | carbs: 6g | net carbs: 4g | fiber: 2g

Chili and Pepper Spiced Beef Stew

Prep time: 15 minutes | Cook time: 1 hour 5 minutes | Serves 4

- 1 onion, chopped
- 2 tablespoons olive oil
- 1 teaspoon ginger paste
- 1 teaspoon coconut amino
- 1 pound (454 g) beef stew meat, cubed
- 1 red bell pepper, seeded and chopped
- ½ scotch bonnet pepper, chopped
- 2 green chilies,
- chopped
- 1 cup tomatoes, chopped
- 1 tablespoon fresh cilantro, chopped
- 1 garlic clove, minced
- ¼ cup vegetable broth
- Salt and black pepper, to taste
- ¼ cup black olives, chopped
- 1 teaspoon jerk seasoning

1. Brown the beef on all sides in warm olive oil over medium heat; remove and set aside.
2. Stir-fry in the red bell peppers, green chilies, jerk seasoning, garlic, scotch bonnet pepper, onion, ginger paste, and coconut amino, for about 5-6 minutes. Pour in the tomatoes and broth, and cook for 1 hour.
3. Stir in the olives, adjust the seasonings and serve sprinkled with fresh cilantro.

Per Serving

Calories: 254 | fat: 12g | protein: 27g | carbs: 11g | net carbs: 9g | fiber: 2g

Sage and Thyme Herbed Lamb Chops

Prep time: 10 minutes | Cook time: 1 hour 10 minutes | Serves 6

- 6 lamb chops
- 1 tablespoon sage
- 1 teaspoon thyme
- 1 onion, sliced
- 1 cup water
- 3 garlic cloves, minced
- 2 tablespoons olive oil
- ½ cup white wine
- Salt and black pepper, to taste

1. Heat the olive oil in a pan. Add onions and garlic, and cook for 4 minutes, until soft. Rub the sage and thyme over the lamb chops.
2. Cook the lamb for about 3 minutes per side. Set aside. Pour the white wine and water into the pan, bring the mixture to a boil.
3. Cook until the liquid is reduced by half. Add the chops in the pan, reduce the heat, and let simmer for 1 hour.

Per Serving

Calories: 215 | fat: 13g | protein: 23g | carbs: 3g | net carbs: 2g | fiber: 1g

Cinnamon Spiced Lamb Kebabs

Prep time: 5 minutes | Cook time: 10 minutes | Serves 4

- 1 pound (454 g) ground lamb
- ¼ teaspoon cinnamon
- 1 egg
- 1 onion, grated
- Salt and ground black pepper, to taste

1. Place all ingredients in a bowl. Mix with your hands to combine well. Divide the meat into 4 pieces. Shape all meat portions around previously-soaked skewers.
2. Preheat grill to medium and grill the kebabs for about 5 minutes per side.

Per Serving

Calories: 246 | fat: 15g | protein: 25g | carbs: 3g | net carbs: 2g | fiber: 1g

Tomato Beef with Thyme leaves

Prep time: 15 minutes | Cook time: 1 hour 48 minutes | Serves 4

- 1 pound (454 g) chuck steak, trimmed and cubed
- 2 tablespoons olive oil
- Salt and black pepper, to taste
- 2 tablespoons almond flour
- 1 medium onion, diced
- ½ cup dry white wine
- 1 red bell pepper, seeded and diced

- 2 teaspoons Worcestershire sauce
- 4 ounces (113 g) tomato purée
- 3 teaspoons smoked
- paprika
- 1 cup beef broth
- Thyme leaves, for garnish

1. First, lightly dredge the meat in the almond flour and set aside. Place a large skillet over medium heat, add 1 tablespoon of oil to heat and then sauté the onion, and bell pepper for 3 minutes. Stir in the paprika, and add the remaining olive oil.

2. Add the beef and cook for 10 minutes in total while turning them halfway. Stir in white wine, let it reduce by half, about 3 minutes, and add Worcestershire sauce, tomato purée, and beef broth.

3. Let the mixture boil for 2 minutes, then reduce the heat to lowest and let simmer for 1½ hours; stirring now and then. Adjust the taste and dish the ragout. Serve garnished with thyme leaves.

Per Serving

Calories: 299 | fat: 17g | protein: 27g | carbs: 11g | net carbs: 9g | fiber: 2g

Beef Salad with Dijon Mustard Dressing

Prep time: 15 minutes | Cook time: 29 minutes | Serves 4

- ½ pound (227 g) rump steak, excess fat trimmed
- 3 green onions, sliced
- 3 tomatoes, sliced
- 1 cup green beans, steamed and sliced
- 2 kohlrabi, peeled and chopped
- ½ cup water
- 2 cups mixed salad greens
- Salt and black pepper, to season

Salad Dressing:

- 2 teaspoons Dijon mustard
- 1 teaspoon erythritol
- Salt and black pepper, to taste
- 3 tablespoons olive oil, plus more for drizzling
- 1 tablespoon red wine vinegar

1. Preheat the oven to 400°F (204°C). Place the kohlrabi on a baking sheet, drizzle with olive oil and bake in the oven for 25 minutes. After cooking, remove, and set aside to cool.

2. In a bowl, mix the Dijon mustard, erythritol, salt, black pepper, vinegar, and olive oil. Set aside.

3. Then, preheat a grill pan over high heat while you season the meat with salt and black pepper. Place the steak in the pan and brown on both sides for 4 minutes each. Remove to rest on a chopping board for 4 more minutes before slicing thinly.

4. In a salad bowl, add green onions, tomatoes, green beans, kohlrabi, salad greens, and steak slices. Drizzle the dressing over and toss with two spoons. Serve the steak salad warm with chunks of low carb bread.

Per Serving

Calories: 232 | fat: 14g | protein: 15g | carbs: 13g | net carbs: 7g | fiber: 6g

Tomato Beef with Zoodles

Prep time: 10 minutes | Cook time: 22 minutes | Serves 5

- 1 pound (454 g) ground beef
- 2 garlic cloves
- 1 onion, chopped
- 1 teaspoon oregano
- 1 teaspoon sage
- 1 teaspoon rosemary
- 7 ounces (198 g) canned chopped tomatoes
- 1 tablespoon olive oil

1. Heat olive oil in a saucepan. Add onion and garlic and cook for 3 minutes. Add beef and cook until browned, about 4-5 minutes.

2. Stir in the herbs and tomatoes. Cook for 15 minutes.

3. Serve with zoodles.

Per Serving

Calories: 216 | fat: 14g | protein: 18g | carbs: 4g | net carbs: 3g | fiber: 1g

Sirloin Skewers and Chopped Scallions

Prep time: 5 minutes | Cook time: 13 minutes | Serves 4

- 1 pound (454 g) sirloin steak, boneless, cubed
- ¼ cup ranch dressing, divided

- Chopped scallions, for garnish

1. Preheat the grill on medium heat to 400°F and thread the beef cubes on the skewers, about 4 to 5 cubes per skewer.

2. Brush half of the ranch dressing on the skewers (all around) and place them on the grill grate to cook for 6 minutes. Turn the skewers once and cook further for 6 minutes.

3. Brush the remaining ranch dressing on the meat and cook them for 1 more minute on each side. Plate, garnish with the scallions, and serve with a mixed veggie salad, and extra ranch dressing.

Per Serving

Calories: 278 | fat: 19g | protein: 24g | carbs: 1g | net carbs: 1g | fiber: 0g

Golden Eggplant Skillet

Prep time: 10 minutes | Cook time: 1 hour | Serves 8

- ½ cup extra-virgin olive oil, divided
- 2 eggs, beaten
- 2 teaspoons salt, divided
- 1 cup shredded Parmesan cheese, divided
- 2½ cups mozzarella cheese, divided
- 2 small eggplants, unpeeled, trimmed
- and cut into ¼-inch rounds
- 1 pound ground beef, preferably grass-fed
- 2 cups whole-milk ricotta cheese
- 2 teaspoons dried basil or oregano
- ¼ teaspoon freshly ground black pepper
- 3 cups Basic Marinara

1. Preheat the oven to 425°F (218°C). Line a baking sheet with aluminum foil and coat with 2 tablespoons of olive oil.

2. In a small, shallow bowl, combine the beaten eggs and 1 teaspoon of salt. In a second bowl, combine ½ cup of Parmesan cheese and ½ cup of mozzarella cheese.

3. One at a time, dredge each eggplant round first in the egg mixture and then in the cheese mixture, coating each side. Place the coated eggplant rounds on the prepared baking sheet and drizzle with 2 tablespoons of olive oil. Bake until golden brown and eggplant is softened, 18 to 20 minutes.

4. While the eggplant bakes, prepare the filling. Heat 2 tablespoons of olive oil in a large skillet over medium heat. Add the ground beef and cook, breaking it apart, until browned and cooked through, 5 to 6 minutes. Do not drain.

5. To the skillet with the beef, stir in the ricotta cheese, basil, remaining 1 teaspoon of salt, and the pepper. Remove from the heat and set aside.

6. In a medium bowl, combine the marinara sauce with the remaining 2 tablespoons of olive oil and whisk until smooth. In a small bowl, combine the remaining 2 cups of mozzarella and ½ cup of Parmesan.

7. Once the eggplant is cooked, assemble the lasagna. Spoon one-third of the sauce mixture into a 9-by-13-inch glass baking dish and spread evenly to coat the bottom.

8. Place half of the eggplant rounds in one layer to fully cover the sauce. Add half of the beef and ricotta mixture on top of the eggplant, spreading evenly. Top with half of the cheese mixture.

9. Repeat another layer with sauce, eggplant, beef and ricotta, and cheese, topping with the final third of the sauce mixture.

10. Bake until the cheese is bubbly and melted, 30 to 35 minutes. Turn the broiler to low and broil until the top is golden brown, about 5 minutes.

11. Remove from the oven and allow to cool slightly before slicing.

Per Serving

Calories: 662 | fat: 51g | protein: 33g | carbs: 17g | net carbs: 11g | fiber: 6g

Cheesy Zucchini Meat Loaf

Prep time: 15 minutes | Cook time: 1 hour | Serves 8

- ½ cup avocado or extra-virgin olive oil, divided
- 2 cups shredded (not spiralized) zucchini, from 2 small or 1 large zucchini
- 1½ teaspoons salt,
- divided
- 1 pound ground beef, preferably grass-fed
- 1 pound ground pork chorizo
- ½ cup chopped cilantro
- ¼ cup chopped

- scallions, green and white parts
- 1 large egg, beaten
- 1 tablespoon chopped chipotle pepper with adobo sauce (see ingredient tip)
- 1 teaspoon garlic

- powder
- ¼ cup almond flour
- 2 cups shredded Mexican cheese blend or cheddar cheese, divided
- 1 tablespoon tomato paste (no sugar added)

1. Preheat the oven to 375°F. Coat a loaf pan with 2 tablespoons of avocado oil.

2. Line a colander with a layer of paper towels and add the shredded zucchini. Sprinkle with ½ teaspoon of salt, tossing to coat. Let sit for 10 minutes, then press down with another layer of paper towels to release some of the excess moisture.

3. While the zucchini drains, in a large bowl, combine the ground beef, chorizo, cilantro, scallions, ¼ cup of oil, egg, chipotle with adobo, garlic powder, and remaining 1 teaspoon of salt. Mix well with a fork.

4. Add the almond flour to the drained zucchini and toss to coat. Add the zucchini to the meat mixture and mix until well combined. Add half of the mixture to the prepared pan and spread evenly. Top with 1 cup of shredded cheese, spreading evenly. Top with the remaining half of the mixture and spread evenly.

5. In a small bowl, whisk together the tomato paste and remaining 2 tablespoons of oil and spread evenly on top of the meat mixture. Sprinkle with the remaining 1 cup of cheese.

6. Bake for 50 to 55 minutes, or until cooked through. Let sit for 10 minutes before cutting.

Per Serving

Calories: 623 | fat: 53g | protein: 33g | carbs: 3g | net carbs: 3g | fiber: 1g

Creamy Cheesy Mushroom Meat Bake

Prep time: 20 minutes | Cook time: 70 minutes | Serves 6

- 4 tablespoons extra-virgin olive oil,
- divided
- 2 cups cauliflower

- florets (from about half a head of cauliflower)
- 2 tablespoons unsalted butter
- ½ cup heavy cream
- 1 cup shredded cheddar cheese
- 2 teaspoons salt, divided
- 2 teaspoons dried thyme, divided
- ½ teaspoon freshly ground black pepper, divided
- 1 pound ground beef, preferably grass-fed
- ½ small yellow onion,

- diced
- 1 cup chopped cabbage
- 1 carrot, peeled and diced
- 2 ribs celery, diced
- 4 ounces mushrooms, sliced
- 4 cloves garlic, minced
- 1 (14½-ounce) can diced tomatoes, with juices
- 2 tablespoons tomato paste
- ½ cup beef stock
- 8 ounces cream cheese, room temperature

1. Heat the oven to 375°F (191°C). Heat 2 tablespoons of olive oil in a medium saucepan over medium-low heat. Add the cauliflower and sauté until just tender, 6 to 8 minutes. Add the butter and heavy cream, cover, reduce heat to low, and cook until cauliflower is very tender, another 6 to 8 minutes. Remove from the heat and allow to cool slightly.

2. Add the cheese, 1 teaspoon of salt, 1 teaspoon of thyme, and ¼ teaspoon of pepper to the cauliflower. Using an immersion blender or hand mixer, puree until very smooth. Set aside.

3. In a large saucepan or skillet, heat the remaining 2 tablespoons of olive oil over medium heat. Add the ground beef and sauté for 5 minutes, breaking apart the meat.

4. Add the onion, cabbage, carrot, celery, and mushrooms and sauté for another 5 to 6 minutes, or until the vegetables are just tender and the meat is browned.

5. Add the garlic, remaining 1 teaspoon of salt, remaining 1 teaspoon of thyme, and remaining ¼ teaspoon of pepper and sauté, stirring, for another 30 seconds.

6. Stir in the tomatoes with their juices and the tomato paste. Bring to a simmer, reduce heat to low, cover, and simmer for 8 to 10 minutes, or until the vegetables are very tender and sauce has

thickened.

7. In a small microwave-safe bowl, combine the stock and cream cheese and microwave on high for 1 minute or until cheese is melted. Whisk until creamy.

8. Add the cream cheese mixture to the meat and vegetables and stir to combine well. Place the mixture in an 8-inch square glass baking dish or pie pan.

9. Spread the pureed cauliflower over the meat mixture and bake until golden, 25 to 30 minutes.

Per Serving

Calories: 868 | fat: 74g | protein: 37g | carbs: 18g | net carbs: 13g | fiber: 5g

Delicious Beef and Tender Broccoli

Prep time: 10 minutes | Cook time: 10 minutes | Serves 4

- ¼ cup beef stock
- ¼ cup low-sodium soy sauce
- ¼ cup sesame oil
- ¼ cup plus 2 tablespoons extra-virgin olive oil, divided
- 4 cloves garlic, minced
- 2 tablespoons chopped fresh ginger
- 1 pound flank steak, sliced against the grain into ¼-inch strips
- 2 cups broccoli florets, cut into bite-size pieces
- ¼ cup minced scallion, green and white parts
- 2 tablespoons sesame seeds

1. In a small bowl, whisk together the stock, soy sauce, sesame oil, ¼ cup of olive oil, the garlic, and ginger.

2. Pour half of the mixture into a large zip-top plastic bag and add the steak slices. Marinate in the refrigerator for at least 1 hour, up to 24 hours.

3. Heat the remaining 2 tablespoons of olive oil in a large skillet over high heat. Remove the steak from the marinade and discard the marinade. Sear the steak for 2 to 3 minutes, until just browned on each side, but not cooked through.

4. Lay four 8-inch squares of aluminum foil on the counter. Place ½ cup of broccoli and a quarter of

the seared steak in the middle of each piece of foil.

5. Pour a quarter of the remaining soy sauce mixture over each steak and broccoli pile, garnish with the scallions and sesame seeds, and cover with a second 8-inch foil square.

6. Fold the foil up to about 1 inch from the mixture on each side. Fold in each corner once to secure and seal the foil pack.

7. Preheat the grill on medium-high heat. Place the prepared foil packs in a single layer on the grill and grill for 6 to 8 minutes or until the steak is cooked through and the broccoli is fork-tender.

Per Serving

Calories: 547 | fat: 46g | protein: 28g | carbs: 7g | net carbs: 5g | fiber: 2g

Tomato Beef Chili

Prep time: 10 minutes | Cook time: 35 minutes | Serves 6

- ¼ cup extra-virgin olive oil
- 1 small yellow onion, diced
- 1 green bell pepper, diced
- 1 pound ground beef, preferably grass-fed
- ½ pound ground Italian sausage (hot or sweet)
- 1 tablespoon chili powder
- 2 teaspoons ground
- cumin
- 1½ teaspoons salt
- 6 cloves garlic, minced
- 1 (14½-ounce) can diced tomatoes, with juices
- 1 (6-ounce) can tomato paste
- 2 cups water
- 2 ripe avocados, pitted, peeled, and chopped
- 1 cup sour cream

1. Heat the olive oil in a large pot over medium heat. Add the onion and bell pepper and sauté for 5 minutes, or until just tender.

2. Add the ground beef and sausage and cook until meat is browned, 5 to 6 minutes, stirring to break into small pieces. Add the chili powder, cumin, salt, and garlic and sauté, stirring frequently, for 1 minute, until fragrant.

3. Add the tomatoes and their juices, tomato paste, and water, stirring to combine well. Bring the mixture to a boil, reduce heat to low, cover, and

simmer for 15 to 20 minutes, stirring occasionally. Add additional water for a thinner chili if desired.

4. Serve hot, garnished with chopped avocado and sour cream.

Per Serving

Calories: 591 | fat: 49g | protein: 25g | carbs: 18g | net carbs: 10g | fiber: 8g

Thyme Herbed Meat Stew

Prep time: 10 minutes | Cook time: 4 to 6 hours | Serves 4

- 1 pound boneless beef short ribs
- 1 teaspoon salt
- ½ teaspoon garlic powder
- ¼ teaspoon freshly ground black pepper
- 4 tablespoons extra-virgin olive oil, divided
- ½ small yellow onion, diced
- 1 carrot, peeled and diced
- 2 ribs celery, diced
- 4 ounces sliced
- mushrooms
- 6 cloves garlic, minced
- 2 teaspoons dried thyme
- 2 teaspoons dried rosemary (or 2 tablespoons fresh)
- 1 teaspoon dried oregano
- 3 cups beef stock
- 1 (14½-ounce) can diced tomatoes, with juices
- ½ cup dry red wine (such as merlot)

1. Season the short ribs with the salt, garlic powder, and pepper.

2. Heat 2 tablespoons of olive oil in a large skillet over high heat. Add the short ribs and brown until dark in color, 2 to 3 minutes per side. Transfer to the bowl of a slow cooker.

3. Add the remaining 2 tablespoons of olive oil to the skillet and reduce heat to medium. Add the onion, carrot, celery, and mushrooms and sauté until just tender but not fully cooked, 3 to 4 minutes. Add the garlic and sauté, stirring, for an additional 30 seconds. Transfer the contents of the skillet to the slow cooker with the ribs.

4. Add the thyme, rosemary, oregano, stock, tomatoes with their juices, and wine, and cook on low for 4 to 6 hours, or until meat are very tender.

5. Remove the ribs from the stew and shred using two forks. Return the shredded meat to the stew and stir to combine well. Serve warm.

Per Serving

Calories: 549 | fat: 43g | protein: 24g | carbs: 14g | net carbs: 9g | fiber: 5g

Baked Blue Cheese Steak

Prep time: 5 minutes | Cook time: 10 minutes | Serves 4

- 4 (4-ounce) filet mignon or New York strip steaks
- 1 teaspoon salt
- 1 teaspoon garlic powder, divided
- ¼ teaspoon freshly ground black pepper
- ¼ cup unsalted butter, room temperature
- ¼ cup crumbled blue cheese
- ½ teaspoon dried thyme
- 2 tablespoons extra-virgin olive oil

1. Preheat the oven to 450°F (232°C). Rub the steaks with the salt, ½ teaspoon of garlic powder, and the pepper. Let sit at room temperature for 15 to 30 minutes.

2. To make the blue cheese butter, in a small bowl, combine the butter, blue cheese, remaining ½ teaspoon of garlic powder, and thyme and whisk until well combined and smooth. Set aside.

3. Heat the olive oil in a large, oven-proof skillet over high heat. When the oil is very hot, add the steaks and sear for 1 minute on each side. Transfer the skillet to the oven and roast to desired doneness.

4. For 1-inch-thick steaks, it will take 3 to 6 minutes for rare (130 to 135°F), 6 to 8 minutes for medium-rare (140 to 155°F), and 8 to 10 minutes for well-done (150 to 155°F). For 1½-inch-thick steaks, cook 4 to 6 minutes for rare and 8 to 10 minutes for well-done.

5. Remove the steaks from the skillet and place each on a separate plate.

6. Top each with 2 tablespoons of blue cheese butter and allow the steak to rest and butter to melt for 5 minutes before serving.

Per Serving

Calories: 437 | fat: 37g | protein: 25g | carbs: 1g | net carbs: 1g | fiber: 0g

Lamb Skewers with Mint Pesto

Prep time: 15 minutes | Cook time: 15 minutes | Serves 4

- 1½ cups fresh mint leaves
- ¼ cup shelled pistachios
- 2 cloves garlic, chopped
- Zest and juice of 1 orange
- ¼ cup sesame oil
- 1 teaspoon salt
- ¼ teaspoon freshly ground black pepper
- ¼ cup extra-virgin olive oil
- ½ cup apple cider vinegar
- 1 pound boneless leg of lamb, cut into 1-inch cubes

1. Combine the mint, pistachios, and garlic in the bowl of a food processor or blender and process until very finely chopped.

2. Add the orange zest and juice, sesame oil, salt, and pepper, and pulse until smooth. With the processor running, stream in the olive oil until smooth.

3. Place ¼ cup of the mint pesto in a small bowl, add the vinegar, and whisk to form a marinade. Place the lamb cubes in the marinade and toss to coat. Cover and refrigerate for at least 1 hour, up to 24 hours.

4. While the lamb is marinating, soak four wooden skewers in water for 30 to 60 minutes. Preheat the oven to 450°F (232°C).

5. Thread the lamb cubes onto the soaked skewers, dividing evenly among the four. Place the skewers on a broiler pan or rimmed baking sheet lined with foil.

6. Cook until browned and cooked through, 12 to 15 minutes, flipping halfway through cooking time.

7. Serve the skewers drizzled with the remaining mint pesto.

Per Serving

Calories: 592 | fat: 52g | protein: 22g | carbs: 5g | net carbs: 4g | fiber: 1g

Cauliflower Sausage Skillet

Prep time: 15 minutes | Cook time: 45 minutes | Serves 4

- 4 cups cauliflower florets (about half of a head), broken or chopped into ½-inch pieces
- ½ cup extra-virgin olive oil, divided
- 1 teaspoon salt, divided
- 8 ounces bulk pork sausage (Italian mild or unsweetened breakfast)
- ½ small onion, diced small
- 4 ribs celery, diced small
- ¼ cup chopped carrot
- (about 1 small carrot)
- 4 ounces chopped mushrooms
- 1 tablespoon fresh sage, finely chopped (or 2 teaspoons dried)
- 1 teaspoon dried thyme
- ¼ teaspoon freshly ground black pepper
- 4 cloves garlic, minced
- 1 cup chicken or vegetable stock
- ¼ cup dry white wine (or additional stock)
- 2 tablespoons fresh parsley, chopped

1. Preheat the oven to 425°F (218°C) and line a rimmed baking sheet with aluminum foil.

2. In a large bowl, toss the cauliflower with ¼ cup of olive oil and ½ teaspoon of salt. Spread the cauliflower in a single layer on the prepared baking sheet, reserving the bowl.

3. Cook the cauliflower until golden brown and crispy but not soft, 10 to 12 minutes. Remove from the oven, reduce heat to 375°F (191°C), and allow the cauliflower to cool slightly before transferring back to the reserved bowl.

4. Heat the remaining ¼ cup of olive oil in a large skillet over medium-high heat.

5. Add the sausage and brown for 10 minutes, breaking it into small pieces. Do not drain the rendered fat.

6. To the skillet with the sausage, add the onion, celery, carrot, mushrooms, sage, thyme, remaining ½ teaspoon of salt, and pepper and sauté until the vegetables begin to soften, 5 to 7 minutes. Add the garlic and sauté, stirring, for another 30 seconds.

7. Add the stock and white wine, increase heat to high, and sauté, continuously stirring, until half

the liquid evaporates.

8. Transfer the sausage-and-vegetable mixture to the bowl with the cauliflower and stir in the parsley. Transfer the mixture to an 8-inch square glass baking dish.

9. Bake uncovered until the top is browned and crispy, 15 to 20 minutes. Allow to rest for 10 minutes before serving.

Per Serving

Calories: 496 | fat: 45g | protein: 12g | carbs: 10g | net carbs: 7g | fiber: 3g

Delicious Meatballs with Spiralized Zucchini

Prep time: 15 minutes | Cook time: 4 hours| Serves 8

- 1 pound ground Italian pork sausage
- 1 pound ground beef, preferably grass-fed
- ½ small yellow onion, minced
- ¼ cup almond flour
- 1 large egg, beaten
- 3 teaspoons Worcestershire sauce, divided
- 2 teaspoons salt, divided
- 1 teaspoon ground allspice
- ½ teaspoon ground

- nutmeg
- ½ teaspoon ground ginger
- ½ teaspoon freshly ground black pepper, divided
- 1½ cups beef stock or broth
- 1 cup heavy cream
- 1 tablespoon Dijon mustard
- 4 ounces cream cheese, room temperature
- 1 cup sour cream, room temperature

1. In a large bowl, combine the pork, beef, onion, almond flour, egg, 1 teaspoon of Worcestershire, 1 teaspoon of salt, the allspice, nutmeg, ginger, and ¼ teaspoon of pepper and mix well with a fork.

2. Form the meat mixture into small 1-inch meatballs, and place on a baking sheet or cutting board.

3. In the bowl of a 5- or 6-quart slow cooker, whisk together the stock, heavy cream, mustard, remaining 2 teaspoons of Worcestershire sauce, remaining 1 teaspoon of salt, and remaining ¼

teaspoon of pepper until smooth and creamy. Place the meatballs in the sauce, trying to not overcrowd. Set the slow cooker to low and cook for 4 hours.

4. After 4 hours of cooking, whisk together the cream cheese and sour cream and add to the warm mixture, gently stirring to incorporate well.

5. Serve the meatballs in their sauce with toothpicks, or over spiralized zucchini for a complete meal. Leftover meatballs and sauce can be frozen for up to 3 months.

Per Serving

Calories: 544 | fat: 49g | protein: 23g | carbs: 5g | net carbs: 4g | fiber: 1g

Sage Herbed Pork Chops with Mushrooms

Prep time: 10 minutes | Cook time: 25 minutes | Serves 4

- 4 tablespoons extra-virgin olive oil, divided
- ½ cup almond flour
- 2 teaspoons dried sage, divided
- 1½ teaspoons salt, divided
- ½ teaspoon freshly ground black pepper, divided
- 1 large egg
- ¼ cup flax meal
- ¼ cup walnuts, very finely chopped

- 4 (4-ounce) boneless pork chops
- 1 tablespoon unsalted butter
- 4 ounces chopped mushrooms
- 2 cloves garlic, minced
- 1 teaspoon dried thyme
- 8 ounces cream cheese, room temperature
- ½ cup heavy cream
- ¼ cup chicken stock

1. Preheat the oven to 400°F (204°C). Line a baking sheet with aluminum foil and coat with 1 tablespoon of olive oil.

2. In a small, shallow bowl, combine the almond flour, 1 teaspoon of sage, ½ teaspoon of salt, and ¼ teaspoon of pepper. In a second small bowl, whisk the egg. In a third small bowl, stir together the flax meal and walnuts.

3. One at a time, dredge each pork chop first in the

flour mixture, then in the egg, then in the flax-and-walnut mixture to fully coat all sides. Place on the prepared baking sheet and drizzle the pork chops evenly with 1 tablespoon of olive oil.

4. Bake until cooked through and golden brown, 18 to 25 minutes, depending on the thickness of the pork.

5. While the pork is baking, prepare the gravy. Heat the remaining 2 tablespoons of olive oil and the butter in a medium saucepan over medium heat. Add the mushrooms and sauté until very tender, 4 to 6 minutes. Add the garlic, remaining 1 teaspoon of sage and 1 teaspoon of salt, thyme, and remaining ¼ teaspoon of pepper, and sauté for an additional 30 seconds.

6. Add the cream cheese to the mushrooms, reduce heat to low, and stir until melted and creamy, 2 to 3 minutes. Whisk in the cream and stock until smooth. Cook over low heat, whisking frequently, until the mixture is thick and creamy, another 3 to 4 minutes.

7. Serve each pork chop covered with a quarter of the mushroom gravy.

Per Serving

Calories: 799 | fat: 69g | protein: 36g | carbs: 11g | net carbs: 7g | fiber: 4g

Chapter 8: Fish and Seafood

Anchovies Cabbage Wraps

Prep time: 10 minutes | Cook time: 0 minutes | Serves 4

- 2 (2-ounce / 57-g) can anchovies in olive oil, drained
- 1 cucumber, sliced
- 2 cups red cabbage, shredded
- 1 red onion, chopped
- 1 teaspoon Dijon
- mustard
- 4 tablespoons mayonnaise
- ¼ teaspoon ground black pepper
- 1 large-sized tomato, diced
- 12 lettuce leaves

1. In a mixing bowl, combine the anchovies with the cucumber, cabbage, onion, mustard, mayonnaise, black pepper, and tomatoes.

2. Arrange the lettuce leaves on a tray. Spoon the anchovy/vegetable mixture into the center of a lettuce leaf, taco-style.

3. Repeat until you run out of ingredients.

Per Serving

Calories: 191 | fat: 13g | protein: 3g | carbs: 10g | net carbs: 7g | fiber: 3g

Cayenne Pepper and Garlic Spiced Shrimp

Prep time: 5 minutes | Cook time: 3 minutes | Serves 5

- 2 tablespoons butter
- 2 cloves garlic, minced
- 2 small cayenne pepper pods
- 2 pounds (907 g)
- shrimp, peeled and deveined
- ¼ cup Manzanilla
- Sea salt and ground black pepper, to taste

1. Melt the butter in a sauté pan over moderate heat. Add the garlic and cayenne peppers and cook for 40 seconds.

2. Add the shrimp and cook for about a minute. Pour in the Manzanilla; season with salt and black pepper.

3. Continue to cook for a minute or so, until the shrimp are cooked through. Add lemon slices to each serving if desired. Enjoy!

Per Serving

Calories: 203 | fat: 6g | protein: 37g | carbs: 2g | net carbs: 2g | fiber: 0g

Citrusy Mixed Fish Stew

Prep time: 15 minutes | Cook time: 6 minutes | Serves 2

- 1 tablespoon olive oil
- 1 shallot, sliced
- 3 garlic cloves, minced
- 1 cup tomato purée
- 5 cups white fish stock
- 1 teaspoon basil
- ½ teaspoon rosemary
- ½ California bay leaf
- ⅓ teaspoon saffron threads, crumbled

- Sea salt and freshly cracked black pepper, to taste
- 1 pound (454 g) grouper fish
- ⅓ pound (151 g)
- cockles, scrubbed
- ⅓ pound (151 g) prawns
- 1 tablespoon fresh lemon juice

1. Heat the olive oil in a stockpot over a moderate flame. Now, sauté the shallot for 3 minutes or until tender; add in the garlic and cook an additional 30 seconds or until aromatic.
2. Pour in the tomato purée and white fish stock; bring everything to a boil. Stir in the basil, rosemary, California bay leaf, saffron threads, salt, and black pepper.
3. Turn the heat to medium-low. Fold in the grouper and cockles; gently stir to combine and allow it to simmer for 2 to 3 minutes. Next, add in the prawns; continue to simmer for 3 minutes more or until everything is thoroughly warmed.
4. Drizzle each serving with fresh lemon juice and enjoy!

Per Serving

Calories: 176 | fat: 5g | protein: 24g | carbs: 5g | net carbs: 4g | fiber: 1g

Dijon Mustard with White Onion

Prep time: 5 minutes | Cook time: 7 minutes | Serves 2

- ¾ pound (340 g) tuna fillet, skinless
- 1 white onion, sliced
- 1 teaspoon Dijon mustard
- 8 Niçoise olives, pitted and sliced
- ½ teaspoon anchovy paste

1. Brush the tuna with nonstick cooking oil; season with salt and freshly cracked black pepper. Then, grill your tuna on a lightly oiled rack approximately 7 minutes, turning over once or twice.
2. Let the fish stand for 3 to 4 minutes and break into bite-sized pieces. Transfer to a nice salad bowl.
3. Toss the tuna pieces with the white onion, Dijon mustard, Niçoise olives, and anchovy paste. Serve

well chilled and enjoy!

Per Serving

Calories: 194 | fat: 3g | protein: 37g | carbs: 1g | net carbs: 1g | fiber: 0g

Hot and Creamy Sea Bass

Prep time: 5 minutes | Cook time: 15 minutes | Serves 4

- 2 teaspoons butter, at room temperature
- ½ white onion, chopped
- 1 tablespoon Old Bay
- seasoning
- ¾ pound (340 g) sea bass, broken into chunks
- 1 cup heavy cream

1. Melt the butter in a soup pot over a moderate flame. Now, sweat the white onion until tender and translucent.
2. Then, add in the Old Bay seasoning and 3 cups of water; bring to a rapid boil. Reduce the heat to medium-low and let it simmer, covered, for 9 to 12 minutes.
3. Fold in the sea bass and heavy cream; continue to cook until everything is thoroughly heated or about 5 minutes. Serve warm and enjoy!

Per Serving

Calories: 257 | fat: 18g | protein: 21g | carbs: 4g | net carbs: 4g | fiber: 0g

Delicious Tilapia Shallots Burgers

Prep time: 5 minutes | Cook time: 46 minutes | Serves 5

- 1½ pounds tilapia fish, broken into chunks
- 2 eggs, whisked
- ½ cup shallots,
- chopped
- ½ cup almond flour
- 1 tablespoon Cajun seasoning mix

1. Mix all of the above ingredients in a bowl. Shape the mixture into 10 patties and place in your refrigerator for about 40 minutes.
2. Cook in the preheated frying pan that is previously greased with nonstick cooking spray.
3. Cook for 3 minutes until golden brown on the

bottom. Carefully flip over and cook the other side for a further 3 minutes. Remove to a paper towel-lined plate until ready to serve.

4. Serve with fresh lettuce, if desired. Bon appétit!

Per Serving

Calories: 238 | fat: 11g | protein: 33g | carbs: 3g | net carbs: 2g | fiber: 1g

Yummy Shrimp Veggie Bowl

Prep time: 5 minutes | Cook time: 20 minutes | Serves 4

- 1 shallot, chopped
- 1 cup ham, cut into 1/2-inch cubes
- 1½ cups tomatoes, crushed
- 1½ cups vegetable broth
- ¾ pound (340 g) shrimp

1. Heat up a lightly greased soup pot over a moderate flame. Now, sauté the shallots until they have softened or about 4 minutes.

2. Add in the ham, tomatoes, and vegetable broth and bring to a boil. Turn the heat to simmer, cover and continue to cook for 13 minutes longer.

3. Fold in the shrimp and continue to simmer until they are thoroughly cooked and the cooking liquid has thickened slightly, about 3 to 4 minutes.

4. Serve in individual bowls and enjoy!

Per Serving

Calories: 170 | fat: 5g | protein: 26g | carbs: 6g | net carbs: 5g | fiber: 1g

Citrusy Herring Spinach Salad

Prep time: 10 minutes | Cook time: 0 minutes | Serves 3

- 6 ounces (170 g) pickled herring pieces, drained and flaked
- ½ cup baby spinach
- 2 tablespoons fresh basil leaves
- 2 tablespoons fresh
- chives, chopped
- 1 teaspoon garlic, minced
- 1 bell pepper, chopped
- 1 red onion, chopped
- 2 tablespoons key lime juice, freshly squeezed

- Sea salt and ground
- black pepper, to taste

1. In a salad bowl, combine the herring pieces with spinach, basil leaves, chives, garlic, bell pepper, and red onion.

2. Then, drizzle key lime juice over the salad; add salt and pepper to taste and toss to combine.

Per Serving

Calories: 134 | fat: 8g | protein: 10g | carbs: 5g | net carbs: 4g | fiber: 1g

One Pan Alaskan Cod Fillet

Prep time: 10 minutes | Cook time: 2 minutes | Serves 4

- 1 tablespoon coconut oil
- 4 Alaskan cod fillets
- Salt and freshly ground black pepper, to taste
- 6 leaves basil, chiffonade Mustard Cream Sauce
- 1 teaspoon yellow mustard
- 1 teaspoon paprika
- ¼ teaspoon ground bay leaf
- 3 tablespoons cream cheese
- ½ cup Greek-style yogurt
- 1 garlic clove, minced
- 1 teaspoon lemon zest
- 1 tablespoon fresh parsley, minced
- Sea salt and ground black pepper, to taste

1. Heat coconut oil in a pan over medium heat. Sear the fish for 2 to 3 minutes per side. Season with salt and ground black pepper.

2. Mix all ingredients for the sauce until everything is well combined. Top the fish fillets with the sauce and serve garnished with fresh basil leaves.

Per Serving

Calories: 166 | fat: 8g | protein: 20g | carbs: 3g | net carbs: 3g | fiber: 0g

Spicy Cheesy Haddock Burgers

Prep time: 10 minutes | Cook time: 6 minutes | Serves 4

- 2 tablespoons extra virgin olive oil
- 8 ounces (227 g) smoked haddock

- 1 egg
- ¼ cup Parmesan cheese, grated
- 1 teaspoon chili powder
- 1 teaspoon dried parsley flakes
- ¼ cup scallions, chopped
- 1 teaspoon fresh garlic, minced
- Salt and ground black pepper, to taste
- 4 lemon wedges

1. Heat 1 tablespoon of oil in a pan over medium-high heat. Cook the haddock for 6 minutes or until just cooked through; discard the skin and bones and flake into small pieces.
2. Mix the smoked haddock, egg, cheese, chili powder, parsley, scallions, garlic, salt, and black pepper in a large bowl.
3. Heat the remaining tablespoon of oil and cook fish burgers until they are well cooked in the middle or about 6 minutes.
4. Garnish each serving with a lemon wedge.

Per Serving

Calories: 174 | fat: 11g | protein: 15g | carbs: 2g | net carbs: 2g | fiber: 0g

Sole Fillet Tomato Stew

Prep time: 5 minutes | Cook time: 20 minutes | Serves 3

- 1 tablespoon butter, at room temperature
- 1 shallot, chopped
- 1 teaspoon curry paste
- 1 cup tomatoes,
- pureed
- ¾ pound (340 g) sole fillets cut into 1-inch pieces

1. Melt the butter in a stockpot over a medium-high flame. Sauté the shallot until softened.
2. Add the curry paste and pureed tomatoes along with 2 cups of water to the pot; bring to a rolling boil.
3. Immediately reduce the heat to medium-low and continue to simmer, covered, for 12 minutes longer; make sure to stir periodically.
4. Fold in the chopped sole fillets; continue to cook for a further 8 minutes or until the fish flakes easily with a fork. Enjoy!

Per Serving

Calories: 191 | fat: 9g | protein: 24g | carbs: 3g | net carbs: 2g | fiber: 1g

Zucchini Fish Bowl

Prep time: 5 minutes | Cook time: 15 minutes | Serves 5

- 2 tablespoons olive oil
- 1 Spanish onion, chopped
- 1 medium-sized zucchini, diced
- 1 vine-ripe tomatoes, pureed
- 1½ pounds (680 g) cod fish fillets

1. Heat the olive oil in a stockpot over medium-high flame. Now, cook the Spanish onion until tender and translucent.
2. Pour in the pureed tomatoes along with 2 cups of water. Bring to a boil and reduce the heat to medium-low. Let it simmer an additional 10 to 13 minutes.
3. Now, fold in the cod fish fillets. Cook, covered, an additional 5 to 6 minutes or until the codfish is just cooked through and an instant-read thermometer registers 140 °F (60°C).
4. Place the fish in individual bowls; ladle the fish broth over each serving, and serve hot. Enjoy.

Per Serving

Calories: 177 | fat: 6g | protein: 25g | carbs: 4g | net carbs: 3g | fiber: 1g

Peppery Bass Fillet

Prep time: 15 minutes | Cook time: 15 minutes | Serves 6

- 2 tablespoons butter, at room temperature
- 1 leek, chopped
- 1 bell pepper, chopped
- 1 serrano pepper, chopped
- 2 garlic cloves, minced
- 2 tablespoons fresh coriander, chopped
- 2 vine-ripe tomatoes,
- pureed
- 4 cups fish stock
- 2 pounds (907 g) sea bass fillets, chopped into small chunks
- 1 tablespoon Old Bay seasoning
- ½ teaspoon sea salt, to taste
- 1 bay laurels

1. Melt the butter in a heavy-bottomed pot over

moderate heat. Stir in the leek and peppers and sauté them for about 5 minutes or until tender.

2. Stir in the garlic and continue to sauté for 30 to 40 seconds more.

3. Add in the remaining ingredients; gently stir to combine. Turn the heat to medium-low and partially cover the pot.

4. Now, let it cook until thoroughly heated, approximately 10 minutes longer. Lastly, discard the bay laurels and serve warm.

Per Serving

Calories: 227 | fat: 8g | protein: 32g | carbs: 5g | net carbs: 4g | fiber: 1g

Marinara Haddock Fillet

Prep time: 5 minutes | Cook time: 10 minutes | Serves 6

- 2 pounds (907 g) haddock fillets
- 1 tablespoon Italian seasoning blend
- Sea salt and freshly
- ground black pepper, to taste
- 2 tablespoons olive oil
- ½ cup marinara sauce

1. Season the haddock fillets and brush them on all sides with olive oil and marinara sauce.

2. Grill over medium heat for 9 to 11 minutes until golden with brown edges.

3. Use a metal spatula to gently lift the haddock fillets, place them on serving plates and serve with the remaining marinara sauce.

Per Serving

Calories: 226 | fat: 6g | protein: 38g | carbs: 2g | net carbs: 1g | fiber: 1g

Chapter 9: Staples, Broths, Sauces and Dressings

Homemade Almond Bread

Prep time: 5 minutes | Cook time: 2 minutes |

Makes 1 Roll

- 1 large egg
- 3 tablespoons almond flour
- 1 tablespoon extra-
- virgin olive oil
- ¼ teaspoon baking powder
- ⅛ teaspoon salt

1. In a microwave-safe ramekin, small bowl, or mug, beat the egg. Add the almond flour, olive oil, baking powder, and salt and mix well with a fork.

2. Microwave on high for 90 seconds.

3. Slide a knife around the edges of the ramekin and flip to remove the bread.

4. Slice the bread in half with a serrated knife if you want to use it to make a sandwich.

Per Serving

Calories: 264 | fat: 24g | protein: 9g | carbs: 4g | net carbs: 2g | fiber: 2g

Sunday Special Fried Rice

Prep time: 10 minutes | Cook time: 10 minutes | Serves 6

- 1 small head cauliflower, bottom stem, leaves, and core removed, and broken into florets
- 1 large egg, beaten
- 1 tablespoon sesame
- oil
- 1 tablespoon soy sauce
- 3 tablespoons coconut oil
- 2 garlic cloves, minced

1. Place the cauliflower florets in a food processor and pulse several times, until the cauliflower is the consistency of rice or couscous.

2. Whisk together the egg, sesame oil, and soy sauce.

3. In a large skillet, heat the coconut oil over medium-high heat. Add the riced cauliflower and sauté, stirring constantly with a spatula, for 3 to 4 minutes, or until starting to brown. Add the garlic and sauté, stirring, for an additional 30 seconds.

4. Add the egg mixture, again stirring constantly, until all the moisture has evaporated and the egg is cooked through, and another 2 to 3 minutes. Remove from the heat and serve immediately.

Per Serving

Calories: 104 | fat: 10g | protein: 2g | carbs: 3g | net

carbs: 2g | fiber: 1g

Citrusy Tahini Hummus

Prep time: 5 minutes | Cook time: 10 minutes | Makes 1 cup

- 1 cup raw cashews
- 2 small cloves garlic, peeled
- 3 tablespoons tahini
- 1 tablespoon lemon juice
- 1 teaspoon salt
- ½ teaspoon smoked paprika
- ¼ cup extra-virgin olive oil

1. Place the cashews in a medium bowl and cover with cold water. Cover the bowl and soak in the refrigerator overnight or up to 24 hours.

2. Drain the water from the cashews and place them in the bowl of a food processor. Add the garlic and tahini and process until smooth but thick.

3. Add the lemon juice, salt, and paprika and pulse until well combined.

4. With the processor running, stream in the olive oil and process until very smooth and silky but not runny. Serve with raw veggies for dipping, such as celery, cucumber, bell pepper, or broccoli.

5. Leftover hummus can be stored in a sealed container in the refrigerator for up to 4 days.

Per Serving

Calories: 199 | fat: 18g | protein: 4g | carbs: 7g | net carbs: 6g | fiber: 1g

Cheesy Garlic Pesto

Prep time: 5 minutes | Cook time: 10 minutes | Makes about 1 cup

- 4 cups packed baby arugula leaves
- 1 cup packed basil leaves
- 1 cup walnuts, chopped
- ½ cup shredded

- Parmesan cheese
- 2 small garlic cloves, peeled and smashed
- ½ teaspoon salt
- ¾ cup extra-virgin olive oil

1. In a food processor, pulse the arugula, basil, walnuts, cheese, and garlic until very finely chopped.

2. Add the salt. With the processor running, stream in the olive oil until well blended and smooth.

3. Transfer the mixture to a glass container and store, tightly covered in the refrigerator, for up to 2 weeks.

Per Serving

Calories: 305 | fat: 32g | protein: 4g | carbs: 4g | net carbs: 3g | fiber: 1g

Choco Peanut Butter Muffins

Prep time: 5 minutes | Cook time: 2 minutes | Makes 16 cup

- ½ cup cacao butter or coconut oil
- ¼ cup unsweetened cocoa powder
- 2 to 4 teaspoons sugar-free sweetener of choice
- ½ teaspoon cinnamon
- ½ teaspoon salt
- ½ cup unsweetened creamy peanut butter or almond butter

1. Line a mini muffin tin with 16 liners. Place the cacao butter and cocoa powder into a microwave-safe bowl and microwave on high for 30 to 45 seconds or until melted. Stir until creamy.

2. Whisk in the sweetener (if using), cinnamon (if using), and salt. Spoon half of the chocolate mixture into the 16 cups, spreading to cover the bottom of the liner. Reserve the other half of the chocolate mixture. Place the pan in the freezer for 10 minutes to set.

3. In a small, microwave-safe bowl, microwave the nut butter for 30 seconds, until soft, and then spread on top of the chocolate in the cups. Freeze for 10 minutes.

4. Microwave the cacao butter mixture for an additional 30 seconds, just to soften it. Dollop the remaining chocolate on top of the nut butter.

5. Return the pan to the freezer and freeze until solid, about 2 hours. Once frozen, peanut butter cups can be transferred to a zip-top bag and stored in the refrigerator for up to 2 weeks or the freezer for up to 3 months.

Per Serving

Calories: 111 | fat: 11g | protein: 2g | carbs: 2g | net carbs: 1g | fiber: 1g

Spicy Marinara Sauce

Prep time: 15 minutes | Cook time: 1 hour | Makes 4 cups

- 2 tablespoons plus ¼ cup extra-virgin olive oil, divided
- 2 tablespoons unsalted butter
- ½ small onion, finely minced
- 2 ribs celery, finely minced
- ¼ cup minced carrot (about 1 small carrot)
- 4 cloves garlic, minced
- 1 teaspoon salt
- ¼ teaspoon freshly
- ground black pepper
- 1 (32-ounce) can crushed tomatoes, with juices
- 2 tablespoons balsamic vinegar
- 1 teaspoon dried oregano
- 1 teaspoon dried rosemary
- ½ to 1 teaspoon red pepper flakes (optional)

1. Heat 2 tablespoons of olive oil and the butter in a medium saucepan over medium heat.
2. Add the onion, celery, and carrot and sauté until just starting to get tender, about 5 minutes. Add the garlic, salt, and pepper and sauté for an additional 30 seconds.
3. Whisk in the tomatoes and their juices, vinegar, remaining ¼ cup of olive oil, oregano, rosemary, and red pepper (if using). Bring to a simmer, cover, reduce heat to low, and simmer for 30 to 60 minutes to allow the flavors to blend.
4. Serve warm. The sauce will keep, tightly covered in the refrigerator, for up to 1 week. Cooled sauce can be frozen for up to 3 months.

Per Serving

Calories: 144 | fat: 13g | protein: 1g | carbs: 6g | net carbs: 3g | fiber: 3g

Curried Coconut Sauce

Prep time: 15 minutes | Cook time: 5 minutes | Makes 2 cups

- 1 (14½-ounce) can
- full-fat coconut milk

- Zest and juice of 1 lime
- 2 tablespoons curry powder
- 1 tablespoon soy sauce
- 1 teaspoon ground
- ginger
- 1 teaspoon garlic powder
- ½ to 1 teaspoon cayenne pepper

1. Whisk all the ingredients in a small saucepan over medium-high heat and bring just below a boil.
2. Remove from heat and allow cooling to room temperature. The sauce will keep, tightly covered in the refrigerator, for up to 1 week.

Per Serving

Calories: 221 | fat: 22g | protein: 3g | carbs: 7g | net carbs: 5g | fiber: 2g

Dill Pickled Mayo Sauce

Prep time: 5 minutes | Cook time: 5 minutes | Makes about ½ cups

- ½ cup mayonnaise
- 2 tablespoons chopped dill pickles (not sweet)
- 1 tablespoon minced red onion
- 1 tablespoon freshly squeezed lemon juice
- ¼ teaspoon salt
- ¼ teaspoon freshly ground black pepper

1. In a small bowl or canning jar, combine all the ingredients and whisk well with a fork.
2. Sauce will store covered in the refrigerator for up to 3 days.

Per Serving

Calories: 95 | fat: 10g | protein: 0g | carbs: 0g | net carbs: 0g | fiber: 0g

Delicious Homemade Red Wine Vinaigrette

Prep time: 5 minutes | Cook time: 10 minutes | Makes 1 cup

- ½ cup extra-virgin olive oil
- ½ cup red wine vinegar
- 1 tablespoon Dijon or stone-ground mustard
- ½ to 1 teaspoon dried herbs such as rosemary, basil, thyme, or oregano (optional)
- ½ teaspoon salt

- ¼ teaspoon freshly ground black pepper

1. In a small bowl or canning jar, combine all the ingredients and whisk or shake until well combined. The dressing will keep, tightly covered in the refrigerator, for up to 2 weeks.
2. Be sure to bring it to room temperature and shake well before serving, as the oil and vinegar will naturally separate.

Per Serving

Calories: 123 | fat: 14g | protein: 0g | carbs: 0g | net carbs: 0g | fiber: 0g

Worcestershire Mayo Caesar Dressing

Prep time: 5 minutes | Cook time: 10 minutes | Makes 1 ½ cup

- 1 cup mayonnaise
- 2 small garlic cloves, pressed with a garlic press (or 1 teaspoon garlic powder)
- 2 tablespoons freshly squeezed lemon juice, from 1 lemon
- 2 teaspoons Dijon mustard
- 1 teaspoon anchovy paste
- 1 teaspoon Worcestershire sauce
- ½ cup freshly grated Parmesan cheese
- ¼ teaspoon salt
- ¼ teaspoon freshly ground black pepper

1. In a canning jar or small bowl, combine the mayonnaise, garlic, lemon juice, mustard, anchovy paste, and Worcestershire and whisk well.
2. Add the cheese, salt, and pepper and whisk until well combined and smooth. The dressing will keep, tightly covered, in the refrigerator, for up to 1 week. Shake or whisk again before serving.

Per Serving

Calories: 145 | fat: 15g | protein: 2g | carbs: 1g | net carbs: 1g | fiber: 0g

Creamy Mayo Poppy Seed Dressing

Prep time: 5 minutes | Cook time: 10 minutes | Makes about 1 cup

- ½ cup mayonnaise
- 2 tablespoons buttermilk, shaken
- 2 tablespoons sour cream
- Zest and juice of 1 small orange (about ¼ cup juice)
- 1 to 2 teaspoons sugar-free sweetener of choice (optional)
- 1 teaspoon dried tarragon
- ½ teaspoon salt
- ¼ teaspoon freshly ground black pepper
- 1 tablespoon poppy seeds

1. In a canning jar or small bowl, combine the mayonnaise, buttermilk, sour cream, orange zest and juice, sweetener (if using), tarragon, salt, and pepper and whisk well.
2. Add the poppy seeds and shake or whisk until well combined and smooth. The dressing will keep covered tightly in the refrigerator for up to 1 week. Shake or whisk again before serving.

Per Serving

Calories: 112 | fat: 11g | protein: 1g | carbs: 2g | net carbs: 2g | fiber: 0g

Chapter 10: Sides and Snacks

Moms Special Deviled Eggs

Prep time: 10 minutes | Cook time: 10 minutes | Serves 4

- 1 tablespoon mayonnaise
- 1 tablespoon extra-virgin olive oil
- 1 teaspoon Dijon mustard
- 1 teaspoon anchovy paste
- ¼ teaspoon freshly ground black pepper
- 4 large hard-boiled eggs, shelled
- 8 pitted green olives, chopped
- 1 tablespoon red onion, minced
- 1 tablespoon fresh parsley, minced

1. In a small bowl, whisk together the mayonnaise, olive oil, mustard, anchovy paste, and pepper. Set aside.
2. Slice the hard-boiled eggs in half lengthwise, remove the yolks, and place the yolks in a medium

3. Smash the yolks well with a fork and stir in the mayonnaise mixture. Add the olives, onion, and parsley and stir to combine.

4. Spoon the filling into each egg white half. Cover and chill for 30 minutes or up to 24 hours before serving cold.

Per Serving

Calories: 137 | fat: 12g | protein: 7g | carbs: 1g | net carbs: 1g | fiber: 0g

Roasted Cauliflower Veggie Bowl

Prep time: 15 minutes | Cook time: 35 minutes | Serves 6

- 6 cups cauliflower florets (1 medium head cauliflower)
- ½ cup extra-virgin olive oil, divided
- 1 teaspoon dried oregano
- ½ teaspoon salt
- ¼ teaspoon freshly ground black pepper
- 10 pitted Kalamata olives, coarsely chopped
- 2 cups baby spinach leaves, coarsely chopped
- ¼ cup fresh parsley leaves, coarsely chopped
- 8 ounces crumbled feta cheese, divided
- 4 ounces goat cheese
- ½ cup heavy cream

1. Preheat the oven to 425°F (218°C).

2. In a large bowl, combine the cauliflower florets, ¼ cup of olive oil, oregano, salt, and pepper and toss to coat well. Transfer to a 9-by-13-inch glass baking dish, reserving the oiled bowl.

3. Roast the cauliflower for 15 to 20 minutes, or until just starting to turn golden brown.

4. Meanwhile, in the same large bowl, combine the olives, spinach, parsley, half the feta, the goat cheese, and the remaining ¼ cup of olive oil. Stir to combine well and incorporate the goat cheese into the mixture.

5. Transfer the hot cauliflower to the large bowl with the olive-and-cheese mixture and toss to coat well. Add the heavy cream and toss again. Transfer back to the baking dish and sprinkle the remaining 4

ounces of feta on top of the vegetables. Return to the oven and roast until bubbly, 10 to 12 minutes. Serve warm.

Per Serving

Calories: 414 | fat: 38g | protein: 12g | carbs: 8g | net carbs: 5g | fiber: 3g

Walnut Brussels Sprouts Bake

Prep time: 10 minutes | Cook time: 40 minutes | Serves 4

- ½ cup walnuts
- 1 pound Brussels sprouts, trimmed and halved
- 6 tablespoons extra-virgin olive oil, divided
- ½ teaspoon salt
- ½ teaspoon garlic powder
- ¼ teaspoon freshly ground black pepper
- 4 ounces pancetta, cut into ½-inch strips
- 2 tablespoons balsamic vinegar

1. Preheat the oven to 425°F (218°C). Place the walnuts on a large baking sheet lined with aluminum foil.

2. Toast the walnuts until just browned and fragrant, but not burned, 3 to 4 minutes. Remove from the oven, roughly chop, and set aside, reserving the foil on the baking sheet.

3. In a large bowl, combine the Brussels sprouts, 4 tablespoons of olive oil, the salt, garlic powder, and pepper and toss to coat well.

4. Transfer the Brussels sprouts to the prepared baking sheet. Do not rinse the bowl.

5. Roast the sprouts for 20 minutes. Remove from the oven, sprinkle with the pancetta, and toss to blend. Return to the oven and roast until the sprouts are golden brown and pancetta is crispy, another 10 to 15 minutes. Remove from the oven and return to the reserved bowl.

6. Add the chopped toasted walnuts to the warm Brussels sprouts and pancetta, and toss to coat.

7. In a small bowl, whisk together the remaining 2 tablespoons of olive oil and the vinegar and drizzle over the mixture. Toss to coat and serve warm.

Calories: 450 | fat: 41g | protein: 10g | carbs: 14g | net carbs: 9g | fiber: 5g

Garlicky Creamed Spinach

Prep time: 10 minutes | Cook time: 15 minutes | Serves 4

- 4 tablespoons unsalted butter
- ½ small onion, minced
- 4 cloves garlic, minced
- 1 (16-ounce) package frozen spinach (about 4 cups), thawed and drained of excess water
- 4 ounces cream cheese, room temperature
- ½ cup heavy cream
- 1 teaspoon salt
- ¼ teaspoon freshly ground black pepper
- ¼ teaspoon nutmeg (optional)

1. Heat the butter in a medium skillet over low heat. Add the onion and sauté for 3 to 4 minutes, or until starting to turn golden. Add the garlic and sauté for another 1 to 2 minutes, or until fragrant.

2. Add the spinach and sauté for 1 to 2 minutes, or until the water has released.

3. Stir in the softened cream cheese and cook over low heat until melted and well incorporated with the spinach, 2 to 3 minutes.

4. Whisk in the heavy cream, salt, pepper, and nutmeg (if using). Increase heat to medium and cook, whisking constantly, until smooth and creamy, 3 to 4 minutes. Serve warm.

Per Serving

Calories: 342 | fat: 33g | protein: 7g | carbs: 9g | net carbs: 5g | fiber: 4g

Roasted Squash Pumpkin Salad

Prep time: 10 minutes | Cook time: 20 minutes | Serves 8

- 1 cup slivered delicata squash half-moons, about ¼ inch thick (see ingredient tip)
- 6 tablespoons extra-
- virgin olive oil, divided
- 1 teaspoon salt, divided
- 4 cups baby kale or baby spinach leaves
- ¼ cup roasted pumpkin seeds (or pecans or walnuts)
- 1 tablespoon balsamic
- vinegar
- ¼ teaspoon freshly ground black pepper
- 4 ounces goat cheese, crumbled

1. Preheat the oven to 400°F (204°C) and line a rimmed baking sheet with aluminum foil.

2. In a medium bowl, toss together the squash, 2 tablespoons of olive oil, and ½ teaspoon of salt.

3. Spread the squash in a single layer on the prepared baking sheet, reserving the bowl, and roast until golden and tender, 15 to 20 minutes.

4. Meanwhile, place the kale in the reserved bowl. Add the pumpkin seeds. Set aside.

5. In a small bowl, whisk together the remaining 4 tablespoons of olive oil, the remaining ½ teaspoon of salt, the vinegar, and pepper and set aside.

6. When the squash has cooked, remove from the oven and add the warm squash to the greens.

7. Drizzle with the dressing and toss to coat well. Top with goat cheese and serve warm.

Per Serving

Calories: 162 | fat: 15g | protein: 4g | carbs: 4g | net carbs: 4g | fiber: 1g

Bulk Italian Sausage Balls

Prep time: 10 minutes | Cook time: 25 minutes | Makes 2 dozen

- 1 pound bulk Italian sausage (not sweet)
- 1 cup almond flour
- 1½ cups finely shredded cheddar cheese
- 1 large egg
- 2 teaspoons baking
- powder
- 1 teaspoon onion powder
- 1 teaspoon fennel seed (optional)
- ½ teaspoon cayenne pepper (optional)

1. Preheat the oven to 350°F (177°C) and line a rimmed baking sheet with aluminum foil.

2. In a large bowl, combine all the ingredients. Use a fork to mix until well blended.

3. Form the sausage mixture into 1½-inch balls and

place 1 inch apart on the prepared baking sheet.

4. Bake for 20 to 25 minutes, or until browned and cooked through.

Per Serving

Calories: 241 | fat: 21g | protein: 11g | carbs: 3g | net carbs: 2g | fiber: 1g

Cheesy Bacon with Raw Veggies

Prep time: 10 minutes | Cook time: 10 minutes | Serves 6

- 2 ounces bacon (about 4 thick slices)
- 4 ounces cream cheese, room temperature
- ¼ cup mayonnaise
- ¼ teaspoon onion powder
- ¼ teaspoon cayenne pepper (optional)
- 1 cup thick-shredded extra-sharp cheddar cheese
- 2 ounces jarred diced pimentos, drained

1. Chop the raw bacon into ½-inch-thick pieces. Cook in a small skillet over medium heat until crispy, 3 to 4 minutes. Use a slotted spoon to transfer the bacon onto a layer of paper towels. Reserve the rendered fat.

2. In a large bowl, combine the cream cheese, mayonnaise, onion powder, and cayenne (if using), and beat with an electric mixer or by hand until smooth and creamy.

3. Add the rendered bacon fat, cheddar cheese, and pimentos and mix until well combined.

4. Refrigerate for at least 30 minutes before serving to allow flavors to blend. Serve cold with raw veggies such as celery, cucumber, or radish.

Per Serving

Calories: 216 | fat: 20g | protein: 8g | carbs: 2g | net carbs: 2g | fiber: 0g

Spicy Cheesy Spinach Dip

Prep time: 10 minutes | Cook time: 25 minutes | Serves 8

- 4 tablespoons extra-virgin olive oil, divided
- ½ small yellow onion, diced
- 1 cup drained artichoke hearts, chopped (about half of a 14-ounce can)
- 8 ounces frozen spinach, thawed and drained of excess liquid (about 2 cups)
- 1 teaspoon salt
- ½ to 1 teaspoon red pepper flakes
- ½ teaspoon garlic powder
- 8 ounces cream cheese, room temperature
- ½ cup shredded Parmesan cheese, divided
- ½ cup mayonnaise

1. Preheat the oven to 375°F. Drizzle 2 tablespoons of olive oil in an 8-inch square glass baking dish and swirl to coat the bottom and sides.

2. Heat the remaining 2 tablespoons of olive oil in a medium skillet over medium heat. Add the onion and artichoke hearts and sauté for 3 to 4 minutes, or until the onion is soft and lightly browned.

3. Add the spinach, salt, red pepper flakes, and garlic powder and sauté for another 1 to 2 minutes.

4. Add the softened cream cheese and cook, stirring constantly, until cheese is fully melted and well incorporated into the vegetables. Add ¼ cup of Parmesan cheese and stir until melted, another 1 to 2 minutes.

5. Remove the skillet from heat and mix in the mayonnaise. Transfer the mixture to the prepared baking dish, and sprinkle the top with the remaining ¼ cup of Parmesan cheese.

6. Bake uncovered until bubbly and the cheese on the top has melted, 10 to 12 minutes. Serve warm.

Per Serving

Calories: 298 | fat: 29g | protein: 6g | carbs: 6g | net carbs: 3g | fiber: 3g

Super Tasty Pecan Coconut Granola Bars

Prep time: 10 minutes | Cook time: 15 minutes | Makes 16 bars

- ½ cup unsweetened almond butter
- 2 tablespoons coconut oil
- 2 to 4 tablespoons granulated sugar-free sweetener
- 1 egg white

- 1 teaspoon ground cinnamon
- 1 teaspoon vanilla extract
- ¼ teaspoon salt
- 2 tablespoons almond flour
- 1 cup unsweetened coconut flakes
- 1 cup slivered almonds
- 1 cup chopped roasted unsalted pecans
- 1 cup shelled pumpkin seeds

1. Preheat the oven to 350°F (177°C). Line an 8-inch square glass baking dish with parchment paper, letting the paper hang over the sides.

2. In a large glass bowl, combine the almond butter, coconut oil, and sweetener and microwave for 30 seconds, or until the coconut oil is melted.

3. Whisk in the egg white, cinnamon, vanilla extract, and salt until smooth and creamy.

4. Stir in the almond flour, coconut flakes, almonds, pecans, and pumpkin seeds until thoroughly combined.

5. Transfer the mixture into the prepared dish and press down firmly with a spatula to cover the bottom evenly.

6. Bake for 15 minutes, or until crispy and slightly browned around the edges.

7. Allow to cool completely before cutting into 16 bars. Bars can be stored tightly wrapped in the freezer for up to 3 months.

Per Serving

Calories: 215 | fat: 20g | protein: 6g | carbs: 6g | net carbs: 3g | fiber: 3g

Sweet and Yummy Pecan Balls

Prep time: 5 minutes | Cook time: 0 minutes | Makes 8

- ½ cup (1 stick) unsalted butter, room temperature
- ¼ cup granulated sugar-free sweetener
- ½ teaspoon vanilla
- extract
- 1 cup almond flour
- ¾ cup chopped roasted unsalted pecans, divided

1. In a large bowl, use an electric mixer on medium speed to cream together the butter and sweetener until smooth. Add the vanilla and beat well.

2. Add the almond flour and ½ cup of chopped pecans, and stir until well incorporated. Place the mixture in the refrigerator for 30 minutes, or until slightly hardened. Meanwhile, very finely chop the remaining ¼ cup of pecans.

3. Using a spoon or your hands, form the chilled mixture into 8 (1-inch) round balls and place on a baking sheet lined with parchment paper. Roll each ball in the finely chopped pecans, and refrigerate for at least 30 minutes before serving.

4. Store in an airtight container in the refrigerator for up to 1 week or in the freezer for up to 2 months.

Per Serving

Calories: 242 | fat: 25g | protein: 4g | carbs: 4g | net carbs: 1g | fiber: 3g

Choco Chia Pudding

Prep time: 10 minutes | Cook time: 0 minutes | Serves 4

- 1 (14-ounce) can full-fat coconut milk
- ⅓ cup chia seeds
- 1 tablespoon unsweetened cocoa powder
- 2 tablespoons unsweetened almond butter
- 2 to 3 teaspoons granulated sugar-free sweetener of choice (optional)
- ½ teaspoon vanilla extract
- ½ teaspoon almond extract (optional)

1. Combine all the ingredients in a small bowl, whisking well to fully incorporate the almond butter.

2. Divide the mixture between four ramekins or small glass jars.

3. Cover and refrigerate for at least 6 hours, preferably overnight. Serve cold.

Per Serving

Calories: 335 | fat: 31g | protein: 7g | carbs: 13g | net carbs: 6g | fiber: 7g

Chapter 11: Salads

Grilled Garlicky Anchovies

Prep time: 5 minutes | Cook time: 3 minutes | Serves 3

- 6 anchovies, cleaned and deboned
- 1 fresh garlic clove, peeled
- 1 teaspoon Dijon mustard
- 2 egg yolks
- ⅓ cup extra-virgin olive oil

1. Place the anchovies onto a lightly oiled grill pan; place under the grill for 2 minutes. Turn them over and cook for a further minute or so; remove from the grill.
2. Process the garlic, Dijon mustard, egg yolks, and extra-virgin olive oil in your blender. Blend until creamy and uniform.
3. Serve the warm grilled anchovies with the Caesar dressing on the side.

Per Serving

Calories: 449 | fat: 34g | protein: 33g | carbs: 1g | net carbs: 1g | fiber: 0g

Grilled Beef Pecan Salad

Prep time: 15 minutes | Cook time: 20 minutes | Serves 4

- 3 tablespoons olive oil
- ½ pound (227 g) beef rump steak, cut into strips
- Salt and black pepper, to taste
- 1 teaspoon cumin
- A pinch of dried thyme
- 2 garlic cloves, minced
- 4 ounces (113 g) Feta cheese, crumbled
- ½ cup pecans, toasted
- 2 cups spinach
- 1½ tablespoons lemon juice
- ¼ cup fresh mint, chopped

1. Season the beef with salt, 1 tablespoon of olive oil, garlic, thyme, pepper, and cumin. Place on a preheated to medium heat grill, and cook for 10 minutes, flip once.
2. Remove the grilled beef to a cutting board, leave to cool, and slice into strips. Sprinkle the pecans

on a lined baking sheet, place in the oven at 350°F (180°C), and toast for 10 minutes.
3. In a salad bowl, combine the spinach with black pepper, mint, remaining olive oil, salt, lemon juice, Feta cheese, and pecans, and toss well to coat. Top with the beef slices and enjoy.

Per Serving

Calories: 435 | fat: 43.1g | protein: 17.1g | carbs: 5.3g | net carbs: 3.4g | fiber: 1.9g

Mayo Chicken Spanish Pepper Salad

Prep time: 15 minutes | Cook time: 15 minutes | Serves 6

- 1½ pounds (680 g) chicken breasts
- ½ cup dry white wine
- 1 onion, chopped
- 2 Spanish peppers, seeded and chopped
- 1 Spanish naga chili pepper, chopped
- 2 garlic cloves, minced
- 2 cups arugula
- ¼ cup mayonnaise
- 1 tablespoon balsamic vinegar
- 1 tablespoon stone-ground mustard
- Sea salt and freshly ground black pepper, to season

1. Place the chicken breasts in a saucepan. Add the wine to the saucepan and cover the chicken with water. Bring to a boil over medium-high heat.
2. Reduce to a simmer and cook partially covered for 10 to 14 minutes (an instant-read thermometer should register 165°F (74°C)).
3. Transfer the chicken from the poaching liquid to a cutting board; cut into bite-sized pieces and transfer to a salad bowl.
4. Add the remaining ingredients to the salad bowl and gently stir to combine. Serve well chilled.

Per Serving

Calories: 280 | fat: 16.2g | protein: 27.2g | carbs: 4.9g | net carbs: 4.0g | fiber: 0.9g

Chicken Lettuce Salad

Prep time: 10 minutes | Cook time: 15 minutes | Serves 2

- 2 chicken thighs, skinless
- Sea salt and cayenne pepper, to season
- ½ teaspoon Dijon mustard
- 1 tablespoon red wine vinegar
- ¼ cup mayonnaise
- 1 small-sized celery stalk, chopped
- 2 spring onion stalks, chopped
- ½ head Romaine lettuce, torn into pieces
- ½ cucumber, sliced

1. Fry the chicken thighs until thoroughly heated and crunchy on the outside; an instant-read thermometer should read about 165°F (74°C).
2. Discard the bones and chop the meat. Place the other ingredients in a serving bowl and stir until everything is well incorporated.
3. Layer the chopped chicken thighs over the salad. Serve well chilled and enjoy!

Per Serving

Calories: 455 | fat: 29.1g | protein: 40.2g | carbs: 6.6g | net carbs: 2.8g | fiber: 3.8g

Pine Nuts and Arugula Salad

Prep time: 15 minutes | Cook time: 0 minutes | Serves 4

- 6 cups baby arugula
- 1 avocado, diced
- ½ cup cherry tomatoes, halved
- ⅓ cup shaved Parmesan cheese
- ¼ cup thinly sliced red onions
- ¼ cup pili nuts or pine
- nuts
- 3 tablespoons extra-virgin olive oil
- 1 tablespoon red wine vinegar
- 1 small clove garlic, pressed or minced
- Salt and pepper, to taste

1. Place all the salad ingredients in a large bowl and gently toss. In a small bowl, stir together the dressing ingredients.
2. Toss the salad with the dressing right before serving.

Per Serving

Calories: 274 | fat: 23.9g | protein: 8.7g | carbs: 9.0g | net carbs: 4.0g | fiber: 5.0g

Italian Tomato Avocado Salad

Prep time: 10 minutes | Cook time: 0 minutes | Serves 5

- 2 medium tomatoes, each cut into 5 slices
- Coarse salt, to taste
- 6 ounces (170 g) fresh Mozzarella, cut into 10 slices
- 2 avocados, cut into 30 thin slices
- 3 to 4 large basil leaves, chopped, plus
- additional leaves for garnish
- ¼ cup extra-virgin olive oil or avocado oil
- 1 lime, halved
- Ground black pepper, to taste
- Italian seasoning (optional)

1. Lay the tomato slices on a serving plate and sprinkle with salt. On top of each tomato, stack a Mozzarella slice, 3 avocado slices, and some chopped basil.
2. Drizzle with the oil and squeeze some lime juice over the top. Sprinkle with pepper and Italian seasoning, if using.
3. Garnish each stack with a basil leaf, if desired.

Per Serving

Calories: 284 | fat: 25.7g | protein: 7.5g | carbs: 8.0g | net carbs: 3.5g | fiber: 4.5g

Oregano Spiced Cucumber Salad

Prep time: 10 minutes | Cook time: 0 minutes | Serves 5

- 2 medium-large cucumbers
- ½ cup thinly sliced red onions
- 4 ounces (113 g) Feta cheese, crumbled
- Salt and pepper, to taste
- ¼ cup extra-virgin
- olive oil
- 1 tablespoon red wine vinegar
- 1 tablespoon Swerve confectioners'-style sweetener
- ½ teaspoon dried ground oregano

1. Peel the cucumbers as desired and cut in half

lengthwise, then slice. In a medium-sized bowl, toss the cucumbers with the onions. Add the Feta and gently toss to combine.

2. Make the dressing: Place all the ingredients in a small bowl and whisk to combine.

3. Serve right away or place in the refrigerator to chill before serving. To serve, gently toss the salad with the dressing and season to taste with salt and pepper.

Per Serving

Calories: 172 | fat: 15.2g | protein: 4.5g | carbs: 6.5g | net carbs: 3.7g | fiber: 2.8g

Pepper Roasted Asparagus Salad

Prep time: 10 minutes | Cook time: 20 minutes | Serves 3

- 1 pound (454 g) asparagus, trimmed
- ¼ teaspoon ground black pepper
- Flaky salt, to season
- 3 tablespoons sesame seeds
- 1 tablespoon Dijon mustard
- ½ lime, freshly squeezed
- 3 tablespoons extra-virgin olive oil
- 2 garlic cloves, minced
- 1 tablespoon fresh tarragon, snipped
- 1 cup cherry tomatoes, sliced

1. Start by preheating your oven to 400°F (205°C). Spritz a roasting pan with nonstick cooking spray.

2. Roast the asparagus for about 13 minutes, turning the spears over once or twice. Sprinkle with salt, pepper, and sesame seeds; roast an additional 3 to 4 minutes.

3. To make the dressing, whisk the Dijon mustard, lime juice, olive oil, and minced garlic. Chop the asparagus spears into bite-sized pieces and place them in a nice salad bowl.

4. Add the tarragon and tomatoes to the bowl; gently toss to combine. Dress your salad and serve at room temperature. Enjoy!

Per Serving

Calories: 160 | fat: 12.4g | protein: 5.7g | carbs: 6.2g | net carbs: 2.2g | fiber: 4.0g

Citrusy Scallion Chicken Salad

Prep time: 10 minutes | Cook time: 15 minutes | Serves 4

- 2 chicken breasts, skinless and boneless
- ½ teaspoon salt
- 2 bay laurels
- 1 thyme sprig
- 1 rosemary sprig
- 4 scallions, trimmed and thinly sliced
- 1 tablespoon fresh coriander, chopped
- 1 teaspoon Dijon mustard
- 2 teaspoons freshly squeezed lemon juice
- 1 cup mayonnaise, preferably homemade

1. Place all ingredients for the poached chicken in a stockpot; cover with water and bring to a rolling boil.

2. Turn the heat to medium-low and let it simmer for about 15 minutes or until a meat thermometer reads 165°F (74°C).

3. Let the poached chicken cool to room temperature. Cut into strips and transfer to a nice salad bowl.

4. Toss the poached chicken with the salad ingredients; serve well chilled and enjoy!

Per Serving

Calories: 540 | fat: 48.9g | protein: 18.9g | carbs: 3.2g | net carbs: 2.8g | fiber: 0.4g

Mayo Chicken and Seeds Salad

Prep time: 10 minutes | Cook time: 15 minutes | Serves 3

- 1 chicken breast, skinless
- ¼ mayonnaise
- ¼ cup sour cream
- 2 tablespoons Cottage cheese, room temperature
- Salt and black pepper, to taste
- ¼ cup sunflower seeds, hulled and roasted
- ½ avocado, peeled and cubed
- ½ teaspoon fresh garlic, minced
- 2 tablespoons scallions, chopped

1. Bring a pot of well-salted water to a rolling boil. Add the chicken to the boiling water; now, turn off the heat, cover, and let the chicken stand in the hot water for 15 minutes.

2. Then, drain the water; chop the chicken into bite-sized pieces. Add the remaining ingredients and mix well.

3. Place in the refrigerator for at least one hour. Serve well chilled. Enjoy!

Per Serving

Calories: 401 | fat: 35.2g | protein: 16.2g | carbs: 5.7g | net carbs: 2.9g | fiber: 2.8g

Appendix 1 Measurement Conversion Chart

MEASUREMENT CONVERSION CHART

VOLUME EQUIVALENTS(DRY)

US STANDARD	METRIC (APPROXIMATE)
1/8 teaspoon	0.5 mL
1/4 teaspoon	1 mL
1/2 teaspoon	2 mL
3/4 teaspoon	4 mL
1 teaspoon	5 mL
1 tablespoon	15 mL
1/4 cup	59 mL
1/2 cup	118 mL
3/4 cup	177 mL
1 cup	235 mL
2 cups	475 mL
3 cups	700 mL
4 cups	1 L

VOLUME EQUIVALENTS(LIQUID)

US STANDARD	US STANDARD (OUNCES)	METRIC (APPROXIMATE)
2 tablespoons	1 fl.oz.	30 mL
1/4 cup	2 fl.oz.	60 mL
1/2 cup	4 fl.oz.	120 mL
1 cup	8 fl.oz.	240 mL
1 1/2 cup	12 fl.oz.	355 mL
2 cups or 1 pint	16 fl.oz.	475 mL
4 cups or 1 quart	32 fl.oz.	1 L
1 gallon	128 fl.oz.	4 L

TEMPERATURES EQUIVALENTS

FAHRENHEIT(F)	CELSIUS(C) (APPROXIMATE)
225 °F	107 °C
250 °F	120 °C
275 °F	135 °C
300 °F	150 °C
325 °F	160 °C
350 °F	180 °C
375 °F	190 °C
400 °F	205 °C
425 °F	220 °C
450 °F	235 °C
475 °F	245 °C
500 °F	260 °C

WEIGHT EQUIVALENTS

US STANDARD	METRIC (APPROXIMATE)
1 ounce	28 g
2 ounces	57 g
5 ounces	142 g
10 ounces	284 g
15 ounces	425 g
16 ounces (1 pound)	455 g
1.5 pounds	680 g
2 pounds	907 g

Appendix 2 The Dirty Dozen and Clean Fifteen

The Dirty Dozen and Clean Fifteen

The Environmental Working Group (EWG) is a nonprofit, nonpartisan organization dedicated to protecting human health and the environment Its mission is to empower people to live healthier lives in a healthier environment. This organization publishes an annual list of the twelve kinds of produce, in sequence, that have the highest amount of pesticide residue-the Dirty Dozen-as well as a list of the fifteen kinds ofproduce that have the least amount of pesticide residue-the Clean Fifteen.

THE DIRTY DOZEN

- The 2016 Dirty Dozen includes the following produce. These are considered among the year's most important produce to buy organic:

Strawberries	Spinach
Apples	Tomatoes
Nectarines	Bell peppers
Peaches	Cherry tomatoes
Celery	Cucumbers
Grapes	Kale/collard greens
Cherries	Hot peppers

- *The Dirty Dozen list contains two additional itemskale/collard greens and hot peppers-because they tend to contain trace levels of highly hazardous pesticides.*

THE CLEAN FIFTEEN

- The least critical to buy organically are the Clean Fifteen list. The following are on the 2016 list:

Avocados	Papayas
Corn	Kiw
Pineapples	Eggplant
Cabbage	Honeydew
Sweet peas	Grapefruit
Onions	Cantaloupe
Asparagus	Cauliflower
Mangos	

- *Some of the sweet corn sold in the United States are made from genetically engineered (GE) seedstock. Buy organic varieties of these crops to avoid GE produce.*

Made in the USA
Las Vegas, NV
30 December 2024